a

moment

of

calm

First published in Great Britain in 2025 by Laurence King, an imprint of
The Orion Publishing Group Ltd, Carmelite House, 50 Victoria Embankment,
London EC4Y 0DZ

An Hachette UK Company
The authorized representative in the EEA is Hachette Ireland, 8 Castlecourt Centre,
Dublin 15, D15 XTP3, Ireland (email: info@hbgi.ie)

10 9 8 7 6 5 4 3 2 1

Introduction © 2025 Ana Sampson
Illustrations © 2025 Fabian Lavater

The moral right of Ana Sampson to be identified as the author of this work has been
asserted in accordance with the Copyright, Designs and Patents Act of 1988.
All rights reserved. No part of this publication may be reproduced, stored in a
retrieval system, or transmitted in any form or by any means, electronic, mechanical,
photocopying, recording, or otherwise, without the prior permission of both the
copyright owner and the above publisher of this book.

A CIP catalogue record for this book is available from the British Library.

ISBN (Hardback) 978 1 39962 837 2
ISBN (eBook) 978 1 39963 250 8

Senior Editor: Katherine Pitt
Art Director: Liam Relph
Design: Charlotte Abrams-Simpson and Hannah Owens
Senior Production Controller: Sarah Cook

Printed in Great Britain by Clays Ltd, Elcograf, S.p.A.

Front and back cover illustrations: Fabian Lavater

www.laurenceking.com
www.orionbooks.co.uk

a moment of calm

edited by Ana Sampson

Laurence King

introduction   16

january   20
1. Lines for Winter – *Mark Strand*   22
2. Snow-Bound: A Winter Idyl – *John Greenleaf Whittier*   23
3. 'Last year my mind was in a dustbin' – *Rebecca Swift*   24
4. Velvet Shoes – *Elinor Wylie*   25
5. That Silent Evening – *Galway Kinnell*   26
6. The Darkling Thrush – *Thomas Hardy*   28
7. Interior – *Hart Crane*   30
8. The Rime of the Ancient Mariner – *Samuel Taylor Coleridge*   31
9. Old Age – *Caroline Clive*   32
10. Central Park at Dusk – *Sara Teasdale*   33
11. Frost at Midnight – *Samuel Taylor Coleridge*   34
12. After the Winter – *Claude McKay*   35
13. 'How many miles to Babylon?' – *Anonymous*   36
14. Beauty – *Edward Thomas*   37
15. Silver Filigree – *Elinor Wylie*   38
16. The Artist's Life – *Anna Wickham*   39
17. Seal Lullaby – *Rudyard Kipling*   40
18. Sunset – *D. H. Lawrence*   41
19. In the Firelight – *Eugene Field*   42
20. For the Bed at Kelmscott – *William Morris*   43
21. When I Have Fears – *John Keats*   44
22. On Children – *Kahlil Gibran*   45
23. New Every Morning – *Susan Coolidge*   46
24. Sonnet 72 – *Edmund Spenser*   47
25. Deep Peace – *Josephine Royle*   48
26. 'Let there be peace' – *Lemn Sissay*   49
27. Not for That City – *Charlotte Mew*   50
28. The Moon – *Robert Louis Stevenson*   51
29. Ode – *Joseph Addison*   52
30. A Lullaby – *Edgar Albert Guest*   53
31. 'My mind to me a kingdom is' – *Sir Edward Dyer*   54

february 56

1	In the Train – *Sara Teasdale*	58
2	The Fallow Deer at the Lonely House – *Thomas Hardy*	59
3	The Everlasting Voices – *W. B. Yeats*	60
4	Winter Sleep – *Elinor Wylie*	61
5	On a Quiet Conscience – *Charles I*	63
6	'If I can stop one heart from breaking' – *Emily Dickinson*	64
7	The Charm – *Rupert Brooke*	65
8	'When I heard the learn'd astronomer' – *Walt Whitman*	66
9	The Old Astronomer to His Pupil – *Sarah Williams*	67
10	Twinkled to Sleep – *Ursula Bethell*	68
11	Up-Hill – *Christina Rossetti*	69
12	On Imagination – *Phillis Wheatley*	70
13	Whale – *Helen Burke*	71
14	The Sun Rising – *John Donne*	72
15	Love (III) – *George Herbert*	74
16	Waiting Both – *Thomas Hardy*	75
17	'Weep you no more, sad fountains' – *Anonymous*	76
18	Happy the Man – *John Dryden*	77
19	Escape at Bedtime – *Robert Louis Stevenson*	78
20	The Heaven's Gate Mountains – *Li T'ai Po*	79
21	Life – *Henry Van Dyke*	80
22	Childe Harold's Pilgrimage – *George Gordon, Lord Byron*	81
23	The Orange – *Wendy Cope*	82
24	The World – *Henry Vaughan*	83
25	Pax – *D. H. Lawrence*	84
26	Henry IV, Part 1, Act 3, Scene 1 – *William Shakespeare*	85
27	Above the Dock – *T. E. Hulme*	86
28	Evening Song – *Willa Cather*	87
29	If – *Rudyard Kipling*	88

march 90

1. Rock Me to Sleep – *Elizabeth Akers Allen* — 92
2. Ode on Solitude – *Alexander Pope* — 93
3. Evening Solace – *Charlotte Brontë* — 94
4. Andrea del Sarto – *Robert Browning* — 95
5. The Way Planets Talk – *Dom Conlon* — 96
6. The Resolve – *Mary, Lady Chudleigh* — 98
7. 'There was an old woman tossed up in a basket' – *Anonymous* — 99
8. Ode – *Arthur O'Shaughnessy* — 100
9. The Moon – *Sappho* — 101
10. March – *Edward Thomas* — 102
11. '"Hope" is the thing with feathers' – *Emily Dickinson* — 104
12. Essay on Friendship – *Mary Leapor* — 105
13. Invictus – *W. E. Henley* — 106
14. 'Bed is too small for my tiredness' – *Anonymous* — 107
15. Ode to Wisdom – *Elizabeth Carter* — 108
16. Romeo and Juliet Act 3, Scene 2 – *William Shakespeare* — 110
17. To S.M., a Young African Painter, on Seeing His Works – *Phillis Wheatley* — 111
18. 'So, we'll go no more a roving' – *George Gordon, Lord Byron* — 112
19. 'To everything there is a season' – *from Ecclesiastes* — 113
20. Song of a Spirit – *Ann Radcliffe* — 114
21. Magna Est Veritas – *Coventry Patmore* — 115
22. A Psalm of Life – *Henry Wadsworth Longfellow* — 116
23. 'All day I've toiled, but not with pain' – *Emily Brontë* — 117
24. Sowing – *Edward Thomas* — 118
25. 'Golden slumbers kiss your eyes' – *Thomas Dekker* — 119
26. Courage – *Amelia Earhart* — 120
27. 'Care-charming sleep' – *John Fletcher* — 121
28. Moonlight and Gas – *Constance Naden* — 122
29. Prayer (I) – *George Herbert* — 123
30. Tell Good People Good Things – *Salena Godden* — 124
31. Hymn to Diana – *Ben Jonson* — 125

april 126

1	Night – *Sidney Lanier*	128
2	'I think I'd like you better, Star' – *Annette Wynne*	129
3	In Sleep – *Richard Francis Burton*	130
4	A Blessing – *James Wright*	131
5	The Loom of Time – *Anonymous*	132
6	Don't Quit – *John Greenleaf Whittier*	134
7	Forgetfulness – *Hart Crane*	135
8	In the Fields – *Charlotte Mew*	136
9	Paris – *Willa Cather*	137
10	'The same stream of life' – *Rabindranath Tagore*	138
11	Planet Earth – *P. K. Page*	139
12	Paradise Lost – *John Milton*	141
13	'What are heavy?' – *Christina Rossetti*	142
14	A Song in the Night – *George MacDonald*	143
15	A Scherzo (a Shy Person's Wishes) – *Dora Greenwell*	144
16	'In the evening' – *Fenton Johnson*	146
17	'Say not the struggle nought availeth' – *Arthur Hugh Clough*	147
18	'There will come soft rains' – *Sara Teasdale*	148
19	Ode on a Distant Prospect of Eton College – *Thomas Gray*	149
20	The Washing – *Jaan Kaplinski*	150
21	Endymion – *John Keats*	151
22	To Sleep – *Maybury Fleming*	152
23	The Tempest Act 4, Scene 1 – *William Shakespeare*	153
24	Scenes from Life on Earth – *Kathryn Simmonds*	154
25	'If all were rain and never sun' – *Christina Rossetti*	155
26	Bells in the Rain – *Elinor Wylie*	156
27	Night – *William Blake*	157
28	Woods: A Prose Sonnet – *Ralph Waldo Emerson*	159
29	My Voysey Wall-Paper – *Margaret Armour*	160
30	He Wishes for the Cloths of Heaven – *W. B. Yeats*	162

may 164

1. 'All nature has a feeling' – *John Clare* — 166
2. The Happy Heart – *Thomas Dekker* — 167
3. 'Twilight and I went hand in hand' – *Lucy Maud Montgomery* — 168
4. May, 1915 – *Charlotte Mew* — 170
5. In the Forest – *Oscar Wilde* — 171
6. An Evening Prospect – *Ann Eliza Bleecker* — 172
7. Leisure – *W. H. Davies* — 174
8. 'If you look for the truth outside yourself' – *Tung-Shan* — 175
9. The Old Love – *Katharine Tynan* — 176
10. To the Nightingale – *John Donne* — 178
11. Nightingale – *Christian Carstairs* — 179
12. The Nightingale Near the House – *Harold Monro* — 180
13. Good-night – *Edward Thomas* — 181
14. Departed Youth – *Hannah Cowley* — 182
15. The Star – *Jane Taylor* — 184
16. Henry VIII Act 3, Scene 1 – *William Shakespeare* — 185
17. So Much Happiness – *Naomi Shihab Nye* — 186
18. To the Evening Star – *William Blake* — 187
19. The Growth of Love XI – *Archibald Lampman* — 188
20. 'Move eastward, happy earth' – *Alfred, Lord Tennyson* — 189
21. A Nocturnal Reverie – *Anne Finch, Countess of Winchilsea* — 190
22. 'Little birds of the night' – *Stephen Crane* — 191
23. When You Go – *Edwin Morgan* — 192
24. Dream Pedlary – *Thomas Lovell Beddoes* — 193
25. An Hymn to the Evening – *Phillis Wheatley* — 194
26. Peace – *Sara Teasdale* — 195
27. Harbor Dawn – *Lucy Maud Montgomery* — 196
28. 'There is no frigate like a book' – *Emily Dickinson* — 197
29. The Treasure – *Rupert Brooke* — 198
30. Change – *Mary Elizabeth Coleridge* — 199
31. Being but Men – *Dylan Thomas* — 200

june   202

1 Rest and Be Thankful! – At the head of Glencroe –   204
   William Wordsworth
2 Villa Pauline – *Katherine Mansfield*   205
3 Epithalamion – *Edmund Spenser*   206
4 Everything Is Going to Be All Right – *Derek Mahon*   207
5 Yet a Little Sleep – *Robert Fuller Murray*   208
6 A Sleeping Priestess of Aphrodite – *Robert Cameron Rogers*   209
7 'The sun has long been set' – *William Wordsworth*   210
8 Lochan – *Kathleen Jamie*   211
9 There Is a Field – *Rumi*   212
10 Bed in Summer – *Robert Louis Stevenson*   213
11 Ode to Psyche – *John Keats*   214
12 The Lotos-Eaters – *Alfred, Lord Tennyson*   216
13 A Midsummer Night's Dream Act 5, Scene 1 –   217
   William Shakespeare
14 Faithful Pollinator – *Sarah Watkinson*   218
15 When Lilacs Last in the Dooryard Bloom'd – *Walt Whitman*   219
16 The Way Through the Woods – *Rudyard Kipling*   220
17 Villanelle of Sunset – *Ernest Dowson*   221
18 'And death shall have no dominion' – *Dylan Thomas*   222
19 Travelling – *William Wordsworth*   224
20 'Soon will the high Midsummer pomps come on' – *Matthew Arnold*   225
21 The Unknown Bird – *Edward Thomas*   226
22 A Midsummer Night's Dream Act 2, Scene 1 –   228
   William Shakespeare
23 Night – *Augusta Cooper Bristol*   229
24 Boats in the Bay – *Winifred Holtby*   231
25 A Sketch from Nature – *John Tupper*   232
26 'Angel spirits of sleep' – *Robert Bridges*   234
27 'There are no gods' – *D. H. Lawrence*   235
28 Moonlight, Summer Moonlight – *Emily Brontë*   236
29 Gitanjali 24–25 – *Rabindranath Tagore*   237
30 The Pleiades – *Amy Lowell*   238

july

		240
1	High Flight – *John Gillespie Magee, Jr.*	242
2	Hymn to the Moon – *Lady Mary Wortley Montagu*	243
3	Vitae Summa Brevis Spem Nos Vetat Incohare Longam – *Ernest Dowson*	244
4	The New Colossus – *Emma Lazarus*	245
5	Dream Variations – *Langston Hughes*	246
6	The Beds of Fleur-de-lys – *Charlotte Perkins Gilman*	247
7	'Warm summer sun' – *Mark Twain*	248
8	Echoes – *Thomas Moore*	249
9	The Sandman – *Margaret Thomson Janvier*	250
10	Seaweed – *D. H. Lawrence*	252
11	The Kingfisher – *W. H. Davies*	253
12	Hot Sun, Cool Fire – *George Peele*	254
13	Proportion – *Amy Lowell*	255
14	The Sea-Shore – *Letitia Elizabeth Landon*	256
15	A Memory – *Lola Ridge*	258
16	'On the beach at night alone' – *Walt Whitman*	259
17	Sea Slumber-Song – *Roden Berkeley Wriothesley Noel*	260
18	Ebbtide at Sundown – *'Michael Field': Katharine Bradley and Edith Cooper*	261
19	Subway Wind – *Claude McKay*	262
20	'A ship, an isle, a sickle moon' – *James Elroy Flecker*	263
21	A Summer Eve's Vision – *Maria Jane Jewsbury*	264
22	A Summer's Night – *Paul Laurence Dunbar*	265
23	The Hill Summit – *Dante Gabriel Rossetti*	266
24	One Night – *Lizette Woodworth Reese*	267
25	Casa Guidi Windows – *Elizabeth Barrett Browning*	268
26	Moonrise – *Gerard Manley Hopkins*	269
27	Dzoka (Return) – *Belinda Zhawi*	270
28	The Aeolian Harp – *Samuel Taylor Coleridge*	272
29	The Soldier – *Rupert Brooke*	274
30	Meeting at Night – *Robert Browning*	275
31	'Now sleeps the crimson petal' – *Alfred, Lord Tennyson*	276

august 278

1 Fragment of a Sleep-Song – *Sydney Dobell* 280
2 The Peace of Wild Things – *Wendell Berry* 282
3 Titus Andronicus Act 2, Scene 3 – *William Shakespeare* 283
4 Fern Hill – *Dylan Thomas* 284
5 Paper Boats – *Rabindranath Tagore* 286
6 The Recollection – *Percy Bysshe Shelley* 287
7 Silent Noon – *Dante Gabriel Rossetti* 289
8 A Strip of Blue – *Lucy Larcom* 290
9 Yasmin (A Ghazel) – *James Elroy Flecker* 292
10 L'Allegro – *John Milton* 293
11 'The house was quiet and the world was calm' – *Wallace Stevens* 294
12 The Garden – *Andrew Marvell* 295
13 'Time flies' – *Found on an English Sundial* 296
14 A Summer Day – *Joanna Baillie* 297
15 Nightfall in the City of Hyderabad – *Sarojini Naidu* 298
16 O Radiant Dark – *George Eliot* 299
17 High Summer – *Ebenezer Jones* 300
18 'The twilight turns' – *James Joyce* 301
19 Good-night – *Paul Laurence Dunbar* 302
20 The Lake Isle of Innisfree – *W. B. Yeats* 303
21 Twilight Calm – *Christina Rossetti* 304
22 Sleep – *Algernon Charles Swinburne* 307
23 My Bed is a Boat – *Robert Louis Stevenson* 308
24 'Nor rural sights alone, but rural sounds' – *William Cowper* 309
25 Holidays – *Henry Wadsworth Longfellow* 311
26 Verses Written in the Chiosk of the British Palace at Pera – 312
Lady Mary Wortley Montagu
27 The Tempest Act 3, Scene 2 – *William Shakespeare* 313
28 At Set of Sun – *Ella Wheeler Wilcox* 314
29 Evening Song – *Sidney Lanier* 315
30 The Tyger – *William Blake* 316
31 Sleep and Poetry – *John Keats* 317

september 318

1. The Garden of Proserpine – *Algernon Charles Swinburne* — 320
2. Little Boy Blue – *Anonymous* — 321
3. Composed Upon Westminster Bridge, September 3, 1802 – *William Wordsworth* — 322
4. Testimonial – *Rita Dove* — 323
5. Sail Away – *Rabindranath Tagore* — 324
6. The Enviable Isles – *Herman Melville* — 325
7. To the Evening Star – *Thomas Campbell* — 326
8. Wander Song – *Anna Wickham* — 327
9. Nightfall – *'Michael Field': Katharine Bradley and Edith Cooper* — 328
10. 'The moon now rises' – *Henry David Thoreau* — 329
11. 'Rocked in the cradle of the deep' – *Emma Hart Willard* — 330
12. A September Night – *George Marion McClellan* — 331
13. Evenen in the Village – *William Barnes* — 332
14. Elegy Written in a Country Churchyard – *Thomas Gray* — 333
15. The Old Vicarage, Grantchester – *Rupert Brooke* — 334
16. Lycidas – *John Milton* — 335
17. Wind and Silver – *Amy Lowell* — 336
18. 'A boat, beneath a sunny sky' – *Lewis Carroll* — 337
19. Pastoral – *Peter Didsbury* — 338
20. The Fort of Rathangan – *Anonymous* — 339
21. The Swan – *John Gould Fletcher* — 340
22. Autumn Birds – *John Clare* — 341
23. Modern Love – *George Meredith* — 342
24. Canticle – *John F. Deane* — 343
25. Roads – *Amy Lowell* — 344
26. Dog – *Harold Monro* — 346
27. Camomile Tea – *Katherine Mansfield* — 348
28. Moonlit Apples – *John Drinkwater* — 349
29. 'Wynken, Blynken, and Nod' – *Eugene Field* — 350
30. The House of Sleep (extract from *Confessio Amantis*) – *John Gower* — 352

october 354

1	Evensong – *Ridgeley Torrence*	356
2	Dejection: An Ode – *Samuel Taylor Coleridge*	357
3	To Autumn – *John Keats*	358
4	Autumn – *T. E. Hulme*	360
5	Milk for the Cat – *Harold Monro*	361
6	The Fog – *Lola Ridge*	363
7	Audides – *Henri Thomas*	364
8	Philip and Mildred – *Adelaide Anne Procter*	365
9	Written Near a Port on a Dark Evening – *Charlotte Smith*	366
10	Hunter's Moon – *Moya Cannon*	367
11	Autumn River Song: On the Broad Reach – *Li T'ai Po*	368
12	'O come with me' – *Emily Brontë*	369
13	Tonight of Yesterday – *Vona Groarke*	370
14	Evening Quatrains – *Charles Cotton*	371
15	Interim – *Lola Ridge*	373
16	Autumn – *Amy Lowell*	374
17	'Western wind, when wilt thou blow?' – *Anonymous*	375
18	On the Eclipse of the Moon, October 1865 – *Charles Tennyson Turner*	376
19	Ulysses and the Siren – *Samuel Daniel*	377
20	'Blazing in gold and quenching in purple' – *Emily Dickinson*	378
21	Silver – *Walter de la Mare*	379
22	The Poet and His Song – *Paul Laurence Dunbar*	380
23	Lines Composed a Few Miles above Tintern Abbey – *William Wordsworth*	382
24	A Ballad of Dreamland – *Algernon Charles Swinburne*	383
25	She Walks in Beauty – *George Gordon, Lord Byron*	384
26	To Imagination – *Emily Brontë*	385
27	Birch Trees – *John Richard Moreland*	387
28	A Study: At Twilight – *Alice Meynell*	388
29	Son-days – *Henry Vaughan*	389
30	Voices of Unseen Spirits – *Richard Hovey*	390
31	I Am – *John Clare*	392

november 394

1. At the Mid Hour of Night – *Thomas Moore* — 396
2. The Starlit Night – *Gerard Manley Hopkins* — 397
3. Rubric – *Josephine Preston Peabody* — 398
4. A November Daisy – *Henry van Dyke* — 399
5. 'Starlight, star bright' – *Anonymous* — 401
6. The Coming of Good Luck – *Robert Herrick* — 402
7. 'Now winter nights enlarge' – *Thomas Campion* — 403
8. Cat – *Lytton Strachey* — 404
9. Miracles – *Walt Whitman* — 406
10. There Remaineth Therefore a Rest for the People of God – *Christina Rossetti* — 407
11. Santa Filomena – *Henry Wadsworth Longfellow* — 408
12. The Secret Song – *Margaret Wise Brown* — 410
13. Thought – *D. H. Lawrence* — 411
14. Astrophil and Stella: Sonnet 39 – *Philip Sidney* — 412
15. 'I dwell in possibility' – *Emily Dickinson* — 413
16. A Prayer – *St Francis of Assisi* — 414
17. Sonnet 318. On His Blindness – *John Milton* — 415
18. Twenty Gallons of Sleep – *Agnes L. Storrie* — 416
19. The Mermaidens' Vesper-Hymn – *George Darley* — 418
20. To Evening – *William Collins* — 419
21. Old Song – *Traditional, West Africa* — 422
22. To-Night – *Louise Chandler Moulton* — 423
23. The Embankment – *T. E. Hulme* — 424
24. To Sleep – *John Keats* — 425
25. Character of a Happy Life – *Henry Wotton* — 426
26. Safe Sounds – *Carol Ann Duffy* — 428
27. A Summing Up – *Charles Mackay* — 429
28. Imagination – *John Davidson* — 430
29. The Winds of Fate – *Ella Wheeler Wilcox* — 431
30. The Pleasant Dark – *Annette Wynne* — 432

december 434

1 Hamlet Act 1, Scene 1 – *William Shakespeare* 436
2 'I heard a bird sing' – *Oliver Herford* 437
3 The Chronicles of Narnia – *Clare Shaw* 438
4 The Bells – *Edgar Allan Poe* 440
5 Winter – *Gerard Manley Hopkins* 442
6 Speak of the North! – *Charlotte Brontë* 444
7 The Owl and the Pussy-Cat – *Edward Lear* 445
8 The Post-Boy – *William Cowper* 447
9 Late Fragment – *Raymond Carver* 448
10 While We Sleep – *Harold Monro* 449
11 To Music, to Becalm his Fever – *Robert Herrick* 450
12 Desiderata – *Max Ehrmann* 451
13 In the Mid-Midwinter after John Donne's 'A Nocturnal on St Lucy's Day' – *Liz Lochhead* 453
14 The Earthly Paradise – *William Morris* 454
15 A Hope – *Charles Kingsley* 455
16 Ode to Winter – *Gillian Clarke* 456
17 Night – *William Morris* 458
18 Night Rhapsody – *Robert Nichols* 459
19 Deck the Halls – *Traditional* 460
20 O Little Town of Bethlehem – *Phillips Brooks* 461
21 Stopping by Woods on a Snowy Evening – *Robert Frost* 463
22 The Wise Men – *Nancy Anne Miller* 464
23 A Child's Christmas in Wales – *Dylan Thomas* 465
24 A Visit from St Nicholas – *Clement Clarke Moore* 466
25 'It came upon the midnight clear' – *Edmund Hamilton Sears* 468
26 A Winter Evening – *Alexander Pushkin* 470
27 Address to a Child During a Boisterous Winter Evening – *Dorothy Wordsworth* 472
28 The Seasons – *James Thomson* 473
29 I Had a Boat – *Mary Elizabeth Coleridge* 474
30 The Year – *Ella Wheeler Wilcox* 475
31 Auld Lang Syne – *Robert Burns* 476

acknowledgements 478

We scamper through a modern world in which we are all, it seems, expected to fill Kipling's unforgiving minute with much more than 60 seconds' worth of distance run. It's hard – even in those last minutes of the day – to step off the ever-spooling treadmill and indulge ourselves with a few moments of real calm, even though we long to do so. I hope this book, and the verses within it, will prove your passport to a little space of serenity whenever you lift it from the shelf.

> **'Then close thine eyes in peace, and sleep secure,**
> **No sleep so sweet as thine, no rest so sure.'**
> *On a Quiet Conscience* by Charles I (1600–1649)

It has been a delightful task to gather these gorgeous poems. Many of them are explicitly about evening and night, and shoot us into the sleeping skies. Up among the stars, in dark and dizzying vastness, today's petty struggles seem to melt away. We have always felt this, it seems. Moons and planets turn gracefully; stars give out their steadfast gleam. We find space – pun intended – in our minds to contemplate, and to rest. When the distances we travel in imagination are so great, nobody is still running.

> **'Though my soul may set in darkness, it will rise in perfect light;**
> **I have loved the stars too fondly to be fearful of the night.'**
> *The Old Astronomer to His Pupil* by Sarah Williams (1837–1868)

Many of these night sky rhymes are well known to us from childhood, conjuring up memories of sleepily half-remembered friends – owls, pussycats, old ladies with brooms, sailors in the night sky – with soothingly familiar music. Might we not, as we once did, wish upon a star or tell ourselves a bedtime story? Do we not need wishes and stories, now, more than ever?

> **'All night across the dark we steer;**
> **But when the day returns at last,**
> **Safe in my room, beside the pier,**
> **I find my vessel fast.'**

My Bed is a Boat by Robert Louis Stevenson (1850–1894)

Some of these writers offer recipes for a peaceful life. It has little to do with striving and bustle, and nothing at all to do with status and success. It has everything to do with tranquillity and contentment.

> **'My mind to me a kingdom is'**
> Sir Edward Dyer (1543–1607)

I love the thought of these poets composing this sage advice centuries ago. Picture the desk at which they sat, the pen they wielded, the candlelight and the deep, pre-industrial silence around them. With what astonishment might Sir Edward Dyer (1543–1607), John Dryden (1631–1700), Susan Coolidge (1835–1905) or even Charles I (1600–1649) have glimpsed us, pausing our frenetic lives for just a moment, in alien rooms, poring over these pages? How would they feel to know that we are still, even now, taking in their beautiful, wise words to calm our hearts and set our course straight?

> **'Take heart with the day and begin again'**
> *New Every Morning* by Susan Coolidge (1835–1905)

There are hymns here to warm rooms on winter nights, when we light the lamps and hunker down. I hope they kindle warmth for you. These are words composed to bring us ease and coziness, the literary equivalent of a blanket to wrap ourselves in.

> 'The house-dog on his paws outspread
> Laid to the fire his drowsy head'

Snow-Bound: A Winter Idyl by John Greenleaf Whittier (1807–1892)

If we cannot hibernate – however appealing it sometimes seems – we can, through poetry, grant ourselves a few holy minutes each day. We connect in these quiet moments with the poet who set down these thoughts for us, however distant their world and their time might be to ours. Their poems act as a springboard into a reverie that is uniquely our own, and it is a rare and precious gift to hear our own still, small voices, so often buried in the clamour of the raucous everyday.

As the year turns, and the earth slowly awakens, we leave poems about the held breath of a snowy landscape, and look to those celebrating the green beauty of spring, and the easy pleasure it brings. The countryside and coastline have long soothed, inspired and nourished, but for the days when a restorative ramble in the fresh air is off the cards, this book is designed as an ejector seat. Here are songs of balmy evenings and gently rushing waves, and anthems to the perfect blue of a dimming spring sky or a sultry summer night. We might sink beneath the waves to drift with mermaids or drowsy seal pups, we might set sail on the waters of an unruffled loch … A poem and our own imaginations can take us anywhere, in mere moments, without the need for packing or palaver.

> 'There is a peace in the depths of the sea,
> Like the peace that is deep in the heart of me.'

Deep Peace by Josephine Royle (dates unknown)

Each of these poems is an escape hatch, and through it we are able to tumble out of the day's shopping lists and inboxes into a quiet and comfortable place. There are words here of love and leisure, of stars and softness, of coziness and contentment, of all the many thoughts we can gather about us to feel warm and safe. Life moves pretty fast, and so do we. I hope that in these pages, through these words – whether written many centuries ago or in recent years – you are given the gift of stillness, and are soothed.

'Right good is rest.'
For the Bed at Kelmscott by William Morris (1834–1896)

january

1 january

Lines for Winter
Mark Strand (1934–2014)

Tell yourself
as it gets cold and gray falls from the air
that you will go on
walking, hearing
the same tune no matter where
you find yourself –
inside the dome of dark
or under the cracking white
of the moon's gaze in a valley of snow.
Tonight as it gets cold
tell yourself
what you know which is nothing
but the tune your bones play
as you keep going. And you will be able
for once to lie down under the small fire
of winter stars.
And if it happens that you cannot
go on or turn back
and you find yourself
where you will be at the end,
tell yourself
in that final flowing of cold through your limbs
that you love what you are.

2 january

Snow-Bound: A Winter Idyl (extract)
John Greenleaf Whittier (1807–1892)

Shut in from all the world without
We sat the clean-winged hearth about,
Content to let the north-wind roar
In baffled rage at pane and door,
While the red logs before us beat
The frost-line back with tropic heat;
And ever, when a louder blast
Shook beam and rafter as it passed,
The merrier up its roaring draught
The great throat of the chimney laughed,
The house-dog on his paws outspread
Laid to the fire his drowsy head,
The cat's dark silhouette on the wall
A couchant tiger's seemed to fall;
And, for the winter fireside meet,
Between the andirons' straddling feet,
The mug of cider simmered slow,
The apples sputtered in a row,
And, close at hand, the basket stood
With nuts from brown October's wood.
What matter how the night behaved?
What matter how the north-wind raved?
Blow high, blow low, not all its snow
Could quench our hearth-fire's ruddy glow.

3 january

'Last year my mind was in a dustbin'
Rebecca Swift (1964-2017)

Last year my mind was in a dustbin.
Recovery was written off.

I hurled — how I hurled
into space towards no thing,

but now, on a dull January morning
plodding back to work

I want to tear the walls down,
fling open windows.

I want the lighter air on my nose,
the tang-white air in the trees.

Wonder of wonder.
Miracle of miracles.

This ordinary human —
this all-too-common thing.

My heart leaps towards the spring.
My fresh aired brain craves everything.

4 january

Velvet Shoes
Elinor Wylie (1885–1928)

Let us walk in the white snow
   In a soundless space;
With footsteps quiet and slow,
   At a tranquil pace,
   Under veils of white lace.

I shall go shod in silk,
   And you in wool,
White as a white cow's milk,
   More beautiful
   Than the breast of a gull.

We shall walk through the still town
   In a windless peace;
We shall step upon white down,
   Upon silver fleece,
   Upon softer than these.

We shall walk in velvet shoes:
   Wherever we go
Silence will fall like dews
   On white silence below.
   We shall walk in the snow.

5 january

That Silent Evening
Galway Kinnell (1927–2014)

I will go back to that silent evening
when we lay together and talked in low, silent voices,
while outside slow lumps of soft snow
fell, hushing as they got near the ground,
with a fire in the room, in which centuries
of tree went up in continuous ghost-giving-up,
without a crackle, into morning light.
Not until what hastens went slower did we sleep.
When we got home we turned and looked back
at our tracks twining out of the woods,
where the branches we brushed against let fall
puffs of sparkling snow, quickly, in silence,
like stolen kisses, and where the *scritch scritch scritch*
among the trees, which is the sound that dies
inside the sparks from the wedge when the sledge
hits it off centre telling everything inside
it is fire, jumped to a black branch, puffed up
but without arms and so to our eyes lonesome,
and yet also – how could we know this? – *happy!*
in shape of chickadee. Lying still in snow,
not iron-willed, like railroad tracks, willing
not to meet until heaven, but here and there
making slubby kissing stops in the field,
our tracks wobble across the snow their long scratch.
Everything that happens here is really little more,
if even that, than a scratch, too. Words, in our mouths,

are almost ready, already, to bandage the one
whom the *scritch scritch scritch*, meaning *if how when*
we might lose each other, scratches scratches scratches
from this moment to that. Then I will go back
to that silent evening, when the past just managed
to overlap the future, if only by a trace,
and the light doubles and shines
through the dark the sparkling that heavens the earth.

6 january

The Darkling Thrush
Thomas Hardy (1840-1928)

I leant upon a coppice gate
   When Frost was spectre-grey,
And Winter's dregs made desolate
   The weakening eye of day.
The tangled bine-stems scored the sky
   Like strings of broken lyres,
And all mankind that haunted nigh
   Had sought their household fires.

The land's sharp features seemed to be
   The Century's corpse outleant,
His crypt the cloudy canopy,
   The wind his death-lament.
The ancient pulse of germ and birth
   Was shrunken hard and dry,
And every spirit upon earth
   Seemed fervourless as I.

At once a voice arose among
   The bleak twigs overhead
In a full-hearted evensong
   Of joy illimited;
An aged thrush, frail, gaunt, and small,
   In blast-beruffled plume,
Had chosen thus to fling his soul
   Upon the growing gloom.

So little cause for carolings
   Of such ecstatic sound
Was written on terrestrial things
   Afar or night around,
That I could think there trembled through
   His happy good-night air
Some blessed Hope, whereof he knew
   And I was unaware.

7 january

Interior
Hart Crane (1899–1932)

It sheds a shy solemnity,
The lamp in our poor room.
O grey and gold amenity, –
Silence and gentle gloom!

Wide from the world, a stolen hour
We claim, and none may know
How love blooms like a tardy flower
Here in the day's after-glow.

And even should the world break in
With jealous threat and guile,
The world, at last, must bow and win
Our pity and a smile.

8 january

The Rime of the Ancient Mariner (extract)
Samuel Taylor Coleridge (1772–1834)

Beyond the shadow of the ship,
I watched the water-snakes:
They moved in tracks of shining white,
And when they reared, the elfish light
Fell off in hoary flakes.

Within the shadow of the ship
I watched their rich attire:
Blue, glossy green, and velvet black,
They coiled and swam; and every track
Was a flash of golden fire.

O happy living things! no tongue
Their beauty might declare:
A spring of love gushed from my heart,
And I blessed them unaware:
Sure my kind saint took pity on me,
And 1 blessed them unaware.

9 january

Old Age
Caroline Clive (1801–1873)

Thou hast been wrong'd, I think old age;
   Thy sovereign reign comes not in wrath,
Thou call'st us home from pilgrimage,
   Spreadest the seat and clear'st the hearth.

The hopes and fears that shook our youth,
   By thee are turn'd to certainty;
I see my boy become a man,
   I hold my girl's girl on my knee.

Whate'er of good has been, dost thou
   In the departed past make sure;
Whate'er has changed from weal to woe,
   Thy comrade Death stands nigh to cure.

And once or twice in age there shines
   Brief gladness, as when winter weaves
In frosty days o'er naked trees,
   A sudden splendour of white leaves.

The past revives, and thoughts return,
   Which kindled once the youthful breast;
They light us, though no more they burn,
   Then turn to grey and are at rest.

10 january

Central Park at Dusk
Sara Teasdale (1884-1933)

Buildings above the leafless trees
   Loom high as castles in a dream,
While one by one the lamps come out
   To thread the twilight with a gleam.
There is no sign of leaf or bud,
   A hush is over everything –
Silent as women wait for love,
   The world is waiting for the spring.

11 january

Frost at Midnight (extract)
Samuel Taylor Coleridge (1772–1834)

The Frost performs its secret ministry,
Unhelped by any wind. The owlet's cry
Came loud – and hark, again! loud as before.
The inmates of my cottage, all at rest,
Have left me to that solitude, which suits
Abstruser musings: save that at my side
My cradled infant slumbers peacefully.
'Tis calm indeed! so calm, that it disturbs
And vexes meditation with its strange
And extreme silentness. Sea, hill, and wood ...
With all the numberless goings-on of life,
Inaudible as dreams! the thin blue flame
Lies on my low-burnt fire, and quivers not;
Only that film, which fluttered on the grate,
Still flutters there, the sole unquiet thing.
Methinks its motion in this hush of nature
Gives it dim sympathies with me who live,
Making it a companionable form,
Whose puny flaps and freaks the idling Spirit
By its own moods interprets, everywhere
Echo or mirror seeking of itself,
And makes a toy of Thought.

*****

Dear Babe, that sleepest cradled by my side,
Whose gentle breathings, heard in this deep calm,
Fill up the interspersed vacancies
And momentary pauses of the thought!

12 january

After the Winter
Claude McKay (1889–1948)

Some day, when trees have shed their leaves
   And against the morning's white
The shivering birds beneath the eaves
   Have sheltered for the night,
We'll turn our faces southward, love,
   Toward the summer isle
Where bamboos spire the shafted grove
   And wide-mouthed orchids smile.

And we will seek the quiet hill
   Where towers the cotton tree,
And leaps the laughing crystal rill,
   And works the droning bee.
And we will build a cottage there
   Beside an open glade,
With black-ribbed blue-bells blowing near,
   And ferns that never fade.

13 january

'How many miles to Babylon?'
Anonymous

How many miles to Babylon?
   Threescore miles and ten.
Can I get there by candlelight?
   Yes, and back again.
If your heels are nimble and light,
   You may get there by candlelight.

14 january

Beauty
Edward Thomas (1878–1917)

What does it mean? Tired, angry, and ill at ease,
No man, woman, or child alive could please
Me now. And yet I almost dare to laugh
Because I sit and frame an epitaph –
'Here lies all that no one loved of him
And that loved no one.' Then in a trice that whim
Has wearied. But, though I am like a river
At fall of evening while it seems that never
Has the sun lighted it or warmed it, while
Cross breezes cut the surface to a file,
This heart, some fraction of me, happily
Floats through the window even now to a tree
Down in the misting, dim-lit, quiet vale,
Not like a pewit that returns to wail
For something it has lost, but like a dove
That slants unswerving to its home and love.
There I find my rest, as through the dusk air
Flies what yet lives in me: Beauty is there.

15 january

Silver Filigree
Elinor Wylie (1885-1928)

The icicles wreathing
On trees in festoon
Swing, swayed to our breathing:
They're made of the moon.

She's a pale, waxen taper;
And these seem to drip
Transparent as paper
From the flame of her tip.

Molten, smoking a little,
Into crystal they pass;
Falling, freezing, to brittle
And delicate glass.

Each a sharp-pointed flower,
Each a brief stalactite
Which hangs for an hour
In the blue cave of night.

16 january

The Artist's Life
Interpretation
Anna Wickham (1883–1947)

The dreamer found his house
Narrow and stained with years.
The wise man said 'How can this stand!
The tinder walls will fall,
The old roof crush that fool.'

But the garden of the house
Was full of kindly trees,
And brave birds build low nests on little shrubs,
And all small beasts were friends.
At night the marching stars stooped to the house
And in blue brittle light Truth spoke.
A wanton and an old poor man
Strayed to the garden.
And in the charmed shadows, sang
A clear, clean song.
The dreamer laughed, 'Let the house fall!'

17 january

Seal Lullaby
Rudyard Kipling (1865-1936)

Oh! hush thee, my baby, the night is behind us,
   And black are the waters that sparkled so green.
The moon, o'er the combers, looks downward to find us
   At rest in the hollows that rustle between.
Where billow meets billow, there soft be thy pillow;
   Ah, weary wee flipperling, curl at thy ease!
The storm shall not wake thee, nor shark overtake thee,
   Asleep in the arms of the slow-swinging seas.

18 january

Sunset
D. H. Lawrence (1885–1930)

There is a band of dull gold in the west, and say what you like
again and again some god of evening leans out of it
and shares being with me, silkily
all of twilight.

19 january

In the Firelight
Eugene Field (1850–1895)

The fire upon the hearth is low,
   And there is stillness everywhere,
   And, like winged spirits, here and there
The firelight shadows fluttering go.
And as the shadows round me creep,
   A childish treble breaks the gloom,
   And softly from a further room
Comes: 'Now I lay me down to sleep.'

And, somehow, with that little prayer
   And that sweet treble in my ears,
   My thought goes back to distant years,
And lingers with a dear one there;
And as I hear my child's amen,
   My mother's faith comes back to me, –
   Crouched at her side I seem to be;
And mother holds my hands again.

Oh for an hour in that dear place,
   Oh for the peace of that dear time,
   Oh for that childish trust sublime,
Oh for a glimpse of mother's face!
Yet, as the shadows round me creep,
   I do not seem to be alone –
   Sweet magic of that treble tone
And 'Now I lay me down to sleep!'

20 january

For the Bed at Kelmscott
William Morris (1834–1896)

The wind's on the wold
And the night is a-cold,
And Thames runs chill
Twixt mead and hill,
But kind and dear
Is the old house here,
And my heart is warm
Midst winter's harm.
Rest, then and rest,
And think of the best
Twixt summer and spring
When all birds sing
In the town of the tree,
And ye lie in me
And scarce dare move
Lest earth and its love
Should fade away
Ere the full of the day.
I am old and have seen
Many things that have been,
Both grief and peace,
And wane and increase.
No tale I tell
Of ill or well,
But this I say,
Night treadeth on day,
And for worst and best
Right good is rest.

21 january

When I Have Fears
John Keats (1795–1821)

When I have fears that I may cease to be
   Before my pen has gleaned my teeming brain,
Before high-pilèd books, in charact'ry,
   Hold like rich garners the full-ripened grain;
When I behold, upon the night's starred face,
   Huge cloudy symbols of a high romance,
And think that I may never live to trace
   Their shadows, with the magic hand of chance;
And when I feel, fair creature of an hour,
   That I shall never look upon thee more,
Never have relish in the faery power
   Of unreflecting love! – then on the shore
Of the wide world I stand alone, and think
Till Love and Fame to nothingness do sink.

22 january

On Children
Kahlil Gibran (1883–1931)

Your children are not your children.
They are the sons and daughters of Life's longing for itself.
They come through you but not from you,
And though they are with you yet they belong not to you.

You may give them your love but not your thoughts,
For they have their own thoughts.
You may house their bodies but not their souls,
For their souls dwell in the house of tomorrow,
which you cannot visit, not even in your dreams.
You may strive to be like them,
but seek not to make them like you.
For life goes not backward nor tarries with yesterday.

You are the bows from which your children
as living arrows are sent forth.
The archer sees the mark upon the path of the infinite,
and He bends you with His might
that His arrows may go swift and far.
Let your bending in the archer's hand be for gladness;
For even as He loves the arrow that flies,
so He loves also the bow that is stable.

23 january

New Every Morning
Susan Coolidge (1835-1905)

Every day is a fresh beginning,
Listen my soul to the glad refrain.
And, spite of old sorrows
And older sinning,
Troubles forecasted
And possible pain,
Take heart with the day and begin again.

24 january

Sonnet 72 (from *Amoretti*)
Edmund Spenser (c. 1552–1599)

Oft when my spirit doth spread her bolder wings,
   In mind to mount up to the purest sky,
It down is weighed with thought of earthly things
   And clogged with burden of mortality,
   Where when that sovereign beauty it doth spy,
Resembling heaven's glory in her light,
   Drawn with sweet pleasure's bait, it back doth fly,
And unto heaven forgets her former flight.
There my frail fancy, fed with full delight,
   Doth bathe in bliss and mantleth most at ease:
Ne thinks of other heaven, but how it might
   Her heart's desire with most contentment please.
      Heart need not with none other happiness,
      But here on earth to have such heaven's bliss.

25 january

Deep Peace
Josephine Royle (dates unknown)

I belong to the tide,
I belong to the sea,
All of its changing and restless life,
All of its ceaseless and endless strife,
These are a part of me;
But there is a peace in the depths of the sea,
Like the peace that is deep in the heart of me.

26 january

'Let there be peace'
Lemn Sissay (b. 1967)

Let there be peace
So frowns fly away like albatross
And skeletons foxtrot from cupboards,
So war correspondents become travel show presenters
And magpies bring back lost property,
Children, engagement rings, broken things.

Let there be peace
So storms can go out to sea to be
Angry and return to me calm,
So the broken can rise up and dance in the hospitals.
Let the aged Ethiopian man in the grey block of flats
Peer through his window and see Addis before him,
So his thrilled outstretched arms become frames
For his dreams.

Let there be peace
Let tears evaporate to form clouds, cleanse themselves
And fall into reservoirs of drinking water.
Let harsh memories burst into fireworks that melt
In the dark pupils of a child's eyes
And disappear like shoals of silver darting fish,
And let the waves reach the shore with a
Shhhhhhhhhhhhhhh shhhhhhhhhhhhhhh
   Shhhhhhhhhhhhhhhh

27 january

Not for That City
Charlotte Mew (1869–1928)

Not for that city of the level sun,
   Its golden streets and glittering gates ablaze –
   The shadeless, sleepless city of white days,
White nights, or nights and days that are as one –
We weary, when all said, all thought, all done,
   We strain our eyes beyond this dusk to see
   What, from the threshold of eternity
We shall step into. No, I think we shun
The splendour of that everlasting glare,
   The clamour of that never-ending song.
   And if for anything we greatly long,
It is for some remote and quiet stair
   Which winds to silence and a space of sleep
   Too sound for waking and for dreams too deep.

28 january

The Moon
Robert Louis Stevenson (1850-1894)

The moon has a face like the clock in the hall;
She shines on thieves on the garden wall,
On streets and fields and harbour quays,
And birdies asleep in the forks of the trees.

The squalling cat and the squeaking mouse,
The howling dog by the door of the house,
The bat that lies in bed at noon,
All love to be out by the light of the moon.

But all of the things that belong to the day
Cuddle to sleep to be out of her way;
And flowers and children close their eyes
Till up in the morning the sun shall rise.

29 january

Ode
Joseph Addison (1672-1719)

The spacious firmament on high,
With all the blue ethereal sky,
And spangled heav'ns, a shining frame,
Their great original proclaim:
Th' unwearied sun, from day to day,
Does his Creator's power display,
And publishes to every land
The work of an almighty hand.

Soon as the evening shades prevail,
The moon takes up the wondrous tale,
And nightly to the list'ning earth
Repeats the story of her birth:
Whilst all the stars that round her burn,
And all the planets in their turn,
Confirm the tidings as they roll,
And spread the truth from pole to pole.

What though, in solemn silence, all
Move round the dark terrestrial ball?
What though nor real voice nor sound
Amid their radiant orbs be found?
In reason's ear they all rejoice,
And utter forth a glorious voice,
For ever singing, as they shine,
'The hand that made us is divine.'

30 january

A Lullaby
Edgar Albert Guest (1881–1959)

The dream ship is ready, the sea is like gold
And the fairy prince waits in command;
There's a cargo of wonderful dreams in the hold,
For the baby that seeks Slumberland.
There are fairies in pink and good fairies in white,
A watch o'er the baby to keep,
Now the silver sails fill with the breeze of the night,
All aboard, for the Harbour of Sleep!

I pray that no tempest shall ruffle the sea
Through the long night that he is away;
And I pray the good captain will bring him to me
With a smile at the close of the day.
Oh, soft as his breath be the breezes that blow,
And gentle the long waves that sweep
The wonderful ship that is waiting to go
With my babe to the Harbour of Sleep.

Softly, so softly, the ship slips away
With its silver sails catching the breeze,
The stars in the sky seem to twinkle and say
Our watch we will keep o'er the seas.
And never a tempest shall happen this night,
But peace shall slip down on the deep,
Safe and sound shall return, with the coming of light,
Your babe from the Harbour of Sleep.

31 january

'My mind to me a kingdom is'
Sir Edward Dyer (1543–1607)

My mind to me a kingdom is,
   Such present joys therein I find,
That it excels all other bliss
   That world affords or grows by kind.
Though much I want which most would have,
Yet still my mind forbids to crave.

No princely pomp, no wealthy store,
   No force to win the victory,
No wily wit to salve a sore,
   No shape to feed a loving eye;
To none of these I yield as thrall,
For why my mind doth serve for all.

I see how plenty suffers oft,
   And hasty climbers soon do fall;
I see that those which are aloft
   Mishap doth threaten most of all;
They get with toil, they keep with fear:
Such cares my mind could never bear.

Content I live, this is my stay,
   I see no more than may suffice;
I press to bear no haughty sway;
   Look, what I lack my mind supplies.
Lo! thus I triumph like a king,
Content with what my mind doth bring.

Some have too much, but still do crave;
    I have little, and seek no more.
They are but poor, though much they have.
    And I am rich with little store.
They poor, I rich; they beg, I give;
They lack, I leave; they pine, I live.

I laugh not at another's loss;
    I grudge not at another's gain;
No worldly waves my mind can toss;
    My state at one doth still remain.
I fear no foe, I fawn no friend;
I loathe not life, nor dread my end.

Some weigh their pleasure by their lust,
    Their wisdom by their rage of will;
Their treasure is their only trust,
    A cloakèd craft their store of skill:
But all the pleasure that I find
Is to maintain a quiet mind.

My wealth is health and perfect ease,
    My conscience clear my choice defence;
I neither seek by bribes to please,
    Nor by deceit to breed offence.
Thus do I live; thus will I die;
Would all did so as well as I!

february

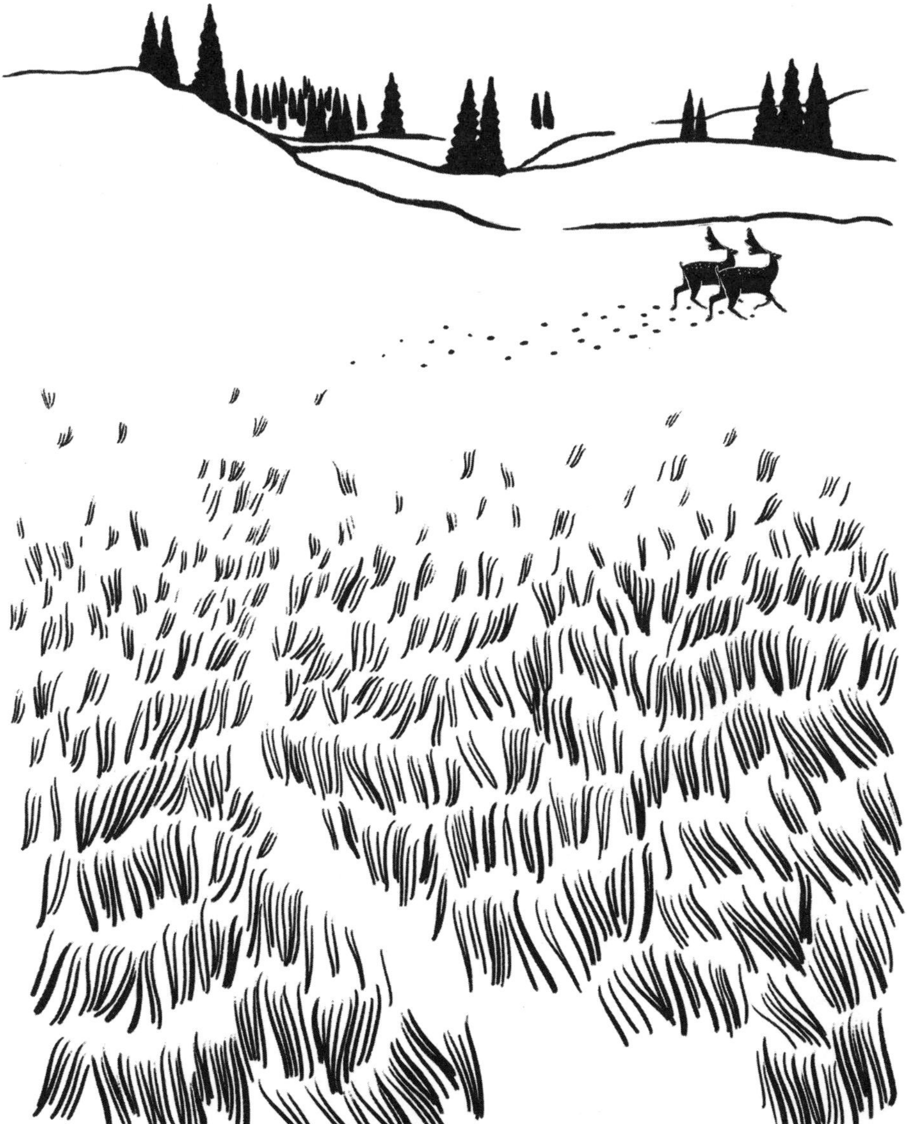

1 february

In the Train
Sara Teasdale (1884-1933)

Fields beneath a quilt of snow
   From which the rocks and stubble peep,
And in the west a shy white star
   That shivers as it wakes from sleep.
The restless rumble of the train,
   The drowsy people in the car,
Steel blue twilight in the world,
   And in my heart a timid star.

2 february

The Fallow Deer at the Lonely House
Thomas Hardy (1840-1928)

One without looks in to-night
    Through the curtain-chink
From the sheet of glistening white;
One without looks in to-night
    As we sit and think
    By the fender-brink.

We do not discern those eyes
    Watching in the snow;
Lit by lamps of rosy dyes
We do not discern those eyes
    Wondering, aglow,
    Fourfooted, tiptoe.

3 february

The Everlasting Voices
W. B. Yeats (1865-1939)

O sweet everlasting Voices, be still;
Go to the guards of the heavenly fold
And bid them wander obeying your will,
Flame under flame, till Time be no more;
Have you not heard that our hearts are old,
That you call in birds, in wind on the hill,
In shaken boughs, in tide on the shore?
O sweet everlasting Voices, be still.

4 february

Winter Sleep
Elinor Wylie (1885–1928)

When against earth a wooden heel
Clicks as loud as stone on steel,
When stone turns flour instead of flakes,
And frost bakes clay as fire bakes,
When the hard-bitten fields at last
Crack like iron flawed in the cast,
When the world is wicked and cross and old,
I long to be quit of the cruel cold.

Little birds like bubbles of glass
Fly to other Americas,
Birds as bright as sparkles of wine
Fly in the night to the Argentine,
Birds of azure and flame-birds go
To the tropical Gulf of Mexico:
They chase the sun, they follow the heat,
It is sweet in their bones, O sweet, sweet, sweet!
It's not with them that I'd love to be,
But under the roots of the balsam tree.

[cont.]

Just as the spiniest chestnut-burr
Is lined within with the finest fur,
So the stoney-walled, snow-roofed house
Of every squirrel and mole and mouse
Is lined with thistledown, sea-gull's feather,
Velvet mullein-leaf, heaped together
With balsam and juniper, dry and curled,
Sweeter than anything else in the world.

O what a warm and darksome nest
Where the wildest things are hidden to rest!
It's there that I'd love to lie and sleep,
Soft, soft, soft, and deep, deep, deep!

5 february

On a Quiet Conscience
Charles I (1600–1649)

Close thine eyes, and sleep secure:
Thy soul is safe, thy body pure.
He that guards thee, He that keeps,
Never slumbers, never sleeps.
A quiet conscience, in a quiet breast
Has only peace, has only rest:
The wisest and the mirth of kings
Are out of tune unless she sings.
Then close thine eyes in peace, and sleep secure,
No sleep so sweet as thine, no rest so sure.

6 february

'If I can stop one heart from breaking'
Emily Dickinson (1830–1886)

If I can stop one heart from breaking
I shall not live in vain;
If I can ease one life the aching,
Or cool one pain,
Or help one fainting robin
Unto his nest again,
I shall not live in vain.

7 february

The Charm (extract)
Rupert Brooke (1887–1915)

In darkness the loud sea makes moan;
And earth is shaken, and all evils creep
About her ways.
   Oh, now to know you sleep!
Out of the whirling blinding moil, alone,
Out of the slow grim fight,
One thought to wing – to you, asleep,
In some cool room that's open to the night
Lying half-forward, breathing quietly,
One white hand on the white
Unrumpled sheet, and the ever-moving hair
Quiet and still at length! . . .

Your magic and your beauty and your strength,
Like hills at noon or sunlight on a tree,
Sleeping prevail in earth and air.

8 february

'When I heard the learn'd astronomer'
Walt Whitman (1819–1892)

When I heard the learn'd astronomer,
When the proofs, the figures, were ranged in columns before me,
When I was shown the charts and diagrams, to add, divide, and
   measure them,
When I sitting heard the astronomer where he lectured with
   much applause in the lecture-room,
How soon unaccountable I became tired and sick,
Till rising and gliding out I wander'd off by myself,
In the mystical moist night-air, and from time to time,
Look'd up in perfect silence at the stars.

9 february

The Old Astronomer to His Pupil (extract)
Sarah Williams (1837–1868)

Though my soul may set in darkness, it will rise in perfect light;
I have loved the stars too fondly to be fearful of the night.

10 february

Twinkled to Sleep
Ursula Bethell (1874–1945)

Cerulean night-sky
    Star-set;
Stygian-dark river-plain
East, north, west,
    Dance-set;
Myriad amber-flashing
Lights dancing, rays flashing, all night.

Delight! delight! Inexpressible heart-dance
    With these.
Strange heart-peace, in sparkling lights!
Blithe heart-ease, starry peace, dancing repose!
Star-charmed, dance-enchanted eyes close,
    Appeased.

Dance in jet-dark depth, in star-set height,
Lights dancing, west, east,
Star-high, heart-deep,
    All night.

11 february

Up-Hill
Christina Rossetti (1830–1894)

Does the road wind up-hill all the way?
   Yes, to the very end.
Will the day's journey take the whole long day?
   From morn to night, my friend.

But is there for the night a resting-place?
   A roof for when the slow, dark hours begin,
May not the darkness hide it from my face?
   You cannot miss that inn.

Shall I meet other wayfarers at night?
   Those who have gone before.
Then must I knock, or call when just in sight?
   They will not keep you standing at that door.

Shall I find comfort, travel-sore and weak?
   Of labour you shall find the sum.
Will there be beds for me and all who seek?
   Yea, beds for all who come.

12 february

On Imagination (extract)
Phillis Wheatley (1753-1784)

Imagination! who can sing thy force?
Or who describe the swiftness of thy course?
Soaring through air to find the bright abode,
Th' empyreal palace of the thund'ring God,
We on thy pinions can surpass the wind,
And leave the rolling universe behind:
From star to star the mental optics rove,
Measure the skies, and range the realms above.
There in one view we grasp the mighty whole,
Or with new worlds amaze th' unbounded soul.

13 february

Whale
Helen Burke (1953–2019)

We discussed
when and where whales sleep
(if they even do). How heavy
is a whale's dream? Maybe it can
only dream once a century. All the rest
of its wide-lipped, big-jawed,
muscle-turned, blink-free day – it fits in,
before tackling its first wink,
its first breath, and its last.
Who could stop a whale doing that?

Its swimming is a graceful egg, a perfect
bowl of white lilies, the pure sound
of a Ming vase.
It does not swim, but pipes the ocean
through its veins, once a day –
turns it in one almighty somersault,
straight up, straight over.
The globe, an aristocrat of acrobats,
is a safe tennis ball in its mouth,
spinning effortlessly – taking
its first breath in with its last,
one long slow breath
before the whale can dream again,
before the Earth should chance to cool –
to spin, to stop.

14 february

The Sun Rising
John Donne (1572–1631)

      Busy old fool, unruly sun,
      Why dost thou thus,
Through windows, and through curtains call on us?
Must to thy motions lovers' seasons run?
      Saucy pedantic wretch, go chide
      Late school-boys, and sour prentices,
   Go tell court-huntsmen, that the King will ride,
   Call country ants to harvest offices;
Love, all alike, no season knows, nor clime,
Nor hours, days, months, which are the rags of time.

      Thy beams, so reverend, and strong
      Why shouldst thou think?
I could eclipse and cloud them with a wink,
But that I would not lose her sight so long:
      If her eyes have not blinded thine,
      Look, and to-morrow late, tell me
   Whether both th'Indias of spice and mine
   Be where thou left'st them, or lie here with me.
Ask for those kings whom thou saw'st yesterday,
And thou shalt hear, 'All here in one bed lay.'

>   She's all states, and all princes, I;
>   Nothing else is.
> Princes do but play us; compared to this,
> All honour's mimic; all wealth alchemy.
>   Thou, sun, art half as happy as we,
>   In that the world's contracted thus;
>   Thine age asks ease, and since thy duties be
>   To warm the world, that's done in warming us.
> Shine here to us, and thou art everywhere;
> This bed thy centre is, these walls, thy sphere.

15 february

Love (III)
George Herbert (1593-1633)

Love bade me welcome. Yet my soul drew back
                Guilty of dust and sin.
But quick-eyed Love, observing me grow slack
                From my first entrance in,
Drew nearer to me, sweetly questioning,
                If I lacked any thing.

A guest, I answered, worthy to be here:
                Love said, You shall be he.
I the unkind, ungrateful? Ah my dear,
                I cannot look on thee.
Love took my hand, and smiling did reply,
                Who made the eyes but I?

Truth Lord, but I have marred them: let my shame
                Go where it doth deserve.
And know you not, says Love, who bore the blame?
                My dear, then I will serve.
You must sit down, says Love, and taste my meat:
                So I did sit and eat.

16 february

Waiting Both
Thomas Hardy (1840-1928)

A star looks down at me,
And says: 'Here I and you
Stand, each in our degree:
What do you mean to do, –
    Mean to do?'

I say: 'For all I know,
Wait, and let Time go by,
Till my change come.' – 'Just so,'
The star says: 'So mean I: –
    So mean I.'

17 february

'Weep you no more, sad fountains'
Anonymous, recorded 1603

    Weep you no more, sad fountains:
      What need you flow so fast?
    Look how the snowy mountains
    Heaven's sun doth gently waste.
      But my sun's heavenly eyes
        View not your weeping,
      That now lies sleeping
      Softly, now softly lies
        Sleeping.

      Sleep is a reconciling,
      A rest that peace begets.
    Doth not the sun rise smiling
      When fair at ev'n he sets?
    Rest you then, rest, sad eyes,
      Melt not in weeping
    While she lies sleeping
    Softly, now softly lies
      Sleeping.

18 february

Happy the Man (extract)
John Dryden (1631-1700)

Happy the man, and happy he alone,
He who can call today his own;
He who, secure within, can say,
Tomorrow, do thy worst, for I have lived today.

19 february

Escape at Bedtime
Robert Louis Stevenson (1850–1894)

The lights from the parlour and kitchen shone out
Through the blinds and the windows and bars;
And high overhead and all moving about,
There were thousands of millions of stars.
There ne'er were such thousands of leaves on a tree,
Nor of people in church or the park,
As the crowds of the stars that looked down upon me,
And that glittered and winked in the dark.

The Dog, and the Plough, and the Hunter, and all,
And the star of the sailor, and Mars,
These shone in the sky, and the pail by the wall
Would be half full of water and stars.
They saw me at last, and they chased me with cries,
And they soon had me packed into bed;
But the glory kept shining and bright in my eyes,
And the stars going round in my head.

20 february

The Heaven's Gate Mountains
Li T'ai Po (701-762), translated by Amy Lowell (1874-1925)

In the far distance, the mountains seem to rise out of the river;
Two peaks, standing opposite each other, make a natural gateway.
The cold colour of the pines is reflected between the river-banks,
Stones divide the current and shiver the wave-flowers to fragments.
Far off, at the border of heaven, is the uneven line of
   mountain-pinnacles;
Beyond, the bright sky is a blur of rose-tinted clouds.
The sun sets, and the boat goes on and on –
As I turn my head, the mountains sink down into the brilliance of
   the cloud-covered sky.

21 february

Life
Henry Van Dyke (1852-1933)

Let me but live my life from year to year,
   With forward face and unreluctant soul;
   Not hurrying to, nor turning from, the goal;
Not mourning for the things that disappear
In the dim past, nor holding back in fear
   From what the future veils; but with a whole
   And happy heart, that pays its toll
To Youth and Age, and travels on with cheer.

So let the way wind up the hill or down,
   O'er rough or smooth, the journey will be joy:
   Still seeking what I sought when but a boy,
New friendship, high adventure, and a crown,
My heart will keep the courage of the quest,
And hope the road's last turn will be the best.

22 february

Childe Harold's Pilgrimage (extract)
George Gordon, Lord Byron (1788–1824)

There is a pleasure in the pathless woods,
There is a rapture on the lonely shore,
There is society, where none intrudes,
By the deep Sea, and music in its roar:
I love not Man the less, but Nature more,
From these our interviews, in which I steal
From all I may be, or have been before,
To mingle with the Universe, and feel
What I can ne'er express, yet cannot all conceal.

23 february

The Orange
Wendy Cope (b. 1945)

At lunchtime I bought a huge orange –
The size of it made us all laugh.
I peeled it and shared it with Robert and Dave –
They got quarters and I had a half.

And that orange, it made me so happy,
As ordinary things often do
Just lately. The shopping. A walk in the park.
This is peace and contentment. It's new.

The rest of the day was quite easy.
I did all the jobs on my list
And enjoyed them and had some time over.
I love you. I'm glad I exist.

24 february

The World (extract)
Henry Vaughan (1621–1695)

I saw eternity the other night,
Like a great ring of pure and endless light,
   All calm as it was bright;
And round beneath it, Time, in hours, days, years,
   Driven by the spheres
Like a vast shadow moved, in which the world
   And all her train were hurled.

25 february

Pax
D. H. Lawrence (1885–1930)

All that matters is to be at one with the living God
to be a creature in the house of the God of Life.

Like a cat asleep on a chair
at peace, in peace
and at one with the master of the house, with the mistress,
at home, at home in the house of the living,
sleeping on the hearth, and yawning before the fire.

Sleeping on the hearth of the living world
yawning at home before the fire of life
feeling the presence of the living God
like a great reassurance
a deep calm in the heart
a presence
as of a master sitting at the board
in his own and greater being,
in the house of life.

26 february

Henry IV, Part 1, Act 3, Scene 1 (extract)
William Shakespeare (c. 1564–1616)

She bids you on the wanton rushes lay you down,
And rest your gentle head upon her lap,
 And she will sing the song that pleaseth you,
And on your eyelids crown the god of sleep,
Charming your blood with pleasing heaviness,
Making such difference 'twixt wake and sleep
As is the difference betwixt day and night,
The hour before the heavenly-harnessed team
Begins his golden progress in the east.

27 february

Above the Dock
T. E. Hulme (1883-1917)

Above the quiet dock in midnight,
Tangled in the tall mast's corded height,
Hangs the moon. What seemed so far away
Is but a child's balloon, forgotten after play.

28 february

Evening Song
Willa Cather (1873–1947)

Dear love, what thing of all the things that be
Is ever worth one thought from you or me,
   Save only Love,
   Save only Love?

The days so short, the nights so quick to flee,
The world so wide, so deep and dark the sea,
   So dark the sea;

So far the suns and every listless star,
Beyond their light – Ah! dear, who knows how far,
   Who knows how far?

One thing of all dim things I know is true,
The heart within me knows, and tells it you,
   And tells it you.

So blind is life, so long at last is sleep,
And none but Love to bid us laugh or weep,
   And none but Love,
   And none but Love.

29 february

If –
Rudyard Kipling (1865–1936)

If you can keep your head when all about you
   Are losing theirs and blaming it on you;
If you can trust yourself when all men doubt you,
   But make allowance for their doubting too;
If you can wait and not be tired by waiting,
   Or being lied about, don't deal in lies,
Or being hated don't give way to hating,
   And yet don't look too good, nor talk too wise;

If you can dream – and not make dreams your master;
   If you can think – and not make thoughts your aim;
If you can meet with Triumph and Disaster
   And treat those two impostors just the same;
If you can bear to hear the truth you've spoken
   Twisted by knaves to make a trap for fools,
Or watch the things you gave your life to, broken,
   And stoop and build 'em up with worn-out tools;

If you can make one heap of all your winnings
   And risk it on one turn of pitch-and-toss,
And lose, and start again at your beginnings
   And never breathe a word about your loss;
If you can force your heart and nerve and sinew
   To serve your turn long after they are gone,
And so hold on when there is nothing in you
   Except the Will which says to them: 'Hold on!'

If you can talk with crowds and keep your virtue,
    Or walk with Kings – nor lose the common touch,
If neither foes nor loving friends can hurt you,
    If all men count with you, but none too much;
If you can fill the unforgiving minute
    With sixty seconds' worth of distance run,
Yours is the Earth and everything that's in it,
    And – which is more – you'll be a Man, my son!

march

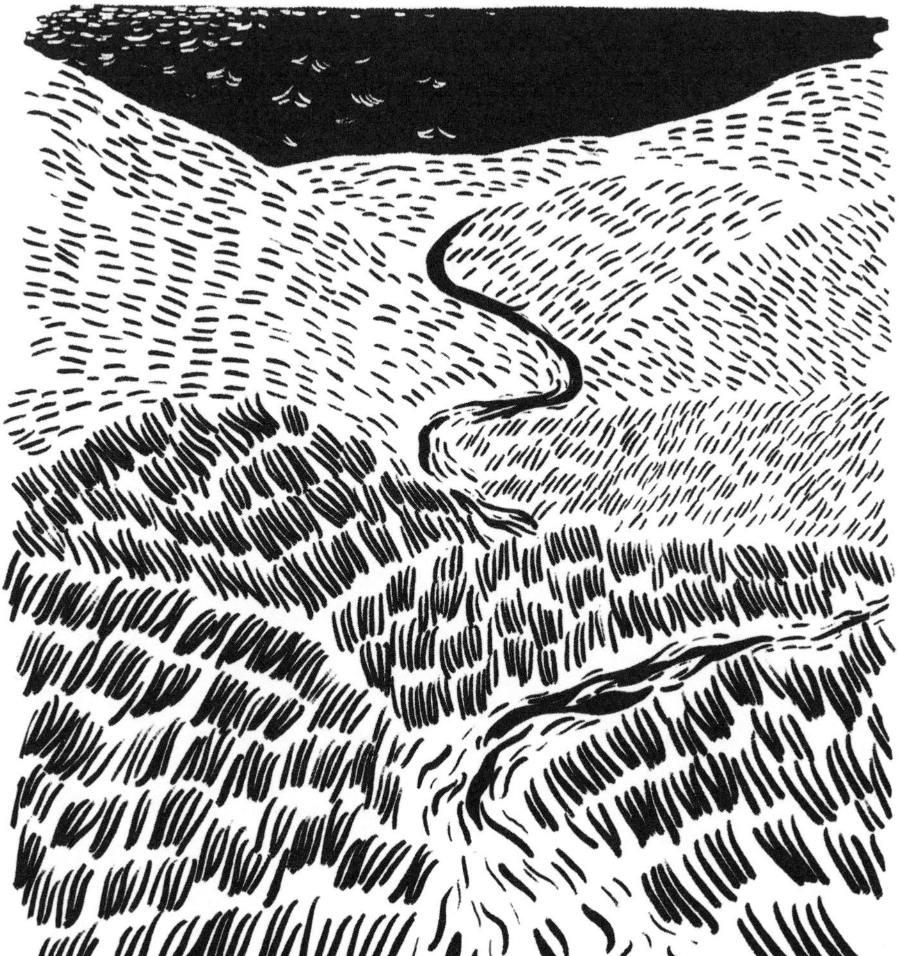

1 march

Rock Me to Sleep (extract)
Elizabeth Akers Allen (1832–1911)

Backward, turn backward, O Time, in your flight,
Make me a child again just for to-night!
Mother, come back from the echoless shore,
Take me again to your heart as of yore;
Kiss from my forehead the furrows of care,
Smooth the few silver threads out of my hair;
Over my slumbers your loving watch keep;
Rock me to sleep, mother – rock me to sleep!

2 march

Ode on Solitude
Alexander Pope (1688–1744)

Happy the man, whose wish and care
   A few paternal acres bound,
Content to breathe his native air,
   In his own ground.

Whose herds with milk, whose fields with bread,
   Whose flocks supply him with attire,
Whose trees in summer yield him shade,
   In winter fire.

Blest, who can unconcern'dly find
   Hours, days, and years slide soft away,
In health of body, peace of mind,
   Quiet by day,

Sound sleep by night; study and ease,
   Together mixed; sweet recreation,
And innocence, which most does please,
   With meditation.

Thus let me live, unseen, unknown;
   Thus unlamented let me die;
Steal from the world, and not a stone
   Tell where I lie.

3 march

Evening Solace (extract)
Charlotte Brontë *(1816–1855)*

The human heart has hidden treasures,
   In secret kept, in silence sealed;
The thoughts, the hopes, the dreams, the pleasures,
   Whose charms were broken if revealed.
And days may pass in gay confusion,
   And nights in rosy riot fly,
While, lost in Fame's or Wealth's illusion,
   The memory of the Past may die.

But there are hours of lonely musing,
   Such as in evening silence come,
When, soft as birds their pinions closing,
   The heart's best feelings gather home.
Then in our souls there seems to languish
   A tender grief that is not woe,
And thoughts that once wrung groans of anguish,
   Now cause but some mild tears to flow.

And feelings, once as strong as passions,
   Float softly back – a faded dream;
Our own sharp griefs and wild sensations,
   The tale of others' sufferings seem.
Oh! when the heart is freshly bleeding,
   How longs it for that time to be,
When, through the mist of years receding,
   Its woes but live in reverie!

4 march

Andrea del Sarto (extract)
Robert Browning *(1812–1889)*

I am grown peaceful as old age tonight.
I regret little, I would change still less.

5 march

The Way Planets Talk
Dom Conlon

What might we hear if we listened
for the star-forged language
the planets used when sound was new
and words had no full stops?

We might hear the distant vowels
of Neptune, each word as long
as life, each sun-abandoned syllable
the sound of a breathing whale.

We might hear the soft lilt of Uranus,
with its dictionary of duck eggs
plopped into blue flour – a thousand
definitions in a single air-thrown sigh.

We might hear the singing voice of Saturn,
with its billion letter alphabet
scattered along a single groove,
its voice recorded in a tantrum of sentences.

We might hear the whirling words of Jupiter,
where 'hello' is the oil in an engine
and 'I love you' is the red echo
of a candle flame dying at sunrise.

We might once have even heard Mars
utter its own name before the words dried
on the tip of its burnt tongue, before
a final, thirst-silenced cry scratched the dust.

We might hear Venus,
Venus who speaks in a dialect
separated from our own
only by a dream on a too-warm night.

And nestled between stone-fist silences
we might hear Mercury
wailing like a boiled baby
each time the sun scrubs its face.

If we listened we might hear these planets,
and take the language from their molten cores
and learn that distance is a comma,
a pause in how we talk about tomorrow.

6 march

The Resolve (extract)
Mary, Lady Chudleigh (1656–1710)

For what the world admires I'll wish no more,
   Nor court that airy nothing of a name:
Such flitting shadows let the proud adore,
   Let them be suppliants for an empty fame.

If Reason rules within, and keeps the throne,
   While the inferior faculties obey,
And all her laws without reluctance own,
   Accounting none more fit, more just than they;

If Virtue my free soul unsullied keeps,
   Exempting it from passion and from stain,
If no black guilty thoughts disturb my sleeps,
   And no past crimes my vexed remembrance pain;

If, though I pleasure find in living here,
   I yet can look on death without surprise;
If I've a soul above the reach of fear,
   And which will nothing mean or sordid prize;

Then am I happy in my humble state,
   Although not crowned with glory nor with bays:
A mind, that triumphs over vice and fate,
Esteems it mean to court the world for praise.

7 march

'There was an old woman tossed up in a basket'
Anonymous

There was an old woman tossed up in a basket,
Seventeen times as high as the moon;
Where she was going I couldn't but ask it,
For in her hand she carried a broom.
Old woman, old woman, old woman, quoth I,
Where are you going to up so high?
To brush the cobwebs off the sky!
May I go with you?
Aye, by-and-by.

8 march

Ode (extract)
Arthur O'Shaughnessy (1844–1881)

We are the music-makers,
And we are the dreamers of dreams,
Wandering by lone sea-breakers,
And sitting by desolate streams;
World-losers and world-forsakers,
Upon whom the pale moon gleams:
Yet we are the movers and shakers
Of the world for ever, it seems.

With wonderful deathless ditties
We build up the world's great cities,
And out of a fabulous story
We fashion an empire's glory:
One man with a dream, at pleasure,
Shall go forth and conquer a crown;
And three with a new song's measure
Can trample an empire down.

We, in the ages lying
In the buried past of the earth,
Built Nineveh with our sighing,
And Babel itself with our mirth;
And o'erthrew them with prophesying
To the old of the new world's worth;
For each age is a dream that is dying,
Or one that is coming to birth.

9 march

The Moon
Sappho (c. 610-570), translated by Edwin Arnold (1832-1904)

The stars about the lovely moon
Fade back and vanish very soon,
When, round and full, her silver face
Swims into sight, and lights all space.

10 march

March
Edward Thomas (1878–1917)

Now I know that Spring will come again,
Perhaps tomorrow: however late I've patience
After this night following on such a day.

While still my temples ached from the cold burning
Of hail and wind, and still the primroses
Torn by the hail were covered up in it,
The sun filled earth and heaven with a great light
And a tenderness, almost warmth, where the hail dripped,
As if the mighty sun wept tears of joy.
But 'twas too late for warmth. The sunset piled
Mountains on mountains of snow and ice in the west:
Somewhere among their folds the wind was lost,
And yet 'twas cold, and though I knew that Spring
Would come again, I knew it had not come,
That it was lost too in those mountains chill.

What did the thrushes know? Rain, snow, sleet, hail,
Had kept them quiet as the primroses.
They had but an hour to sing. On boughs they sang,
On gates, on ground; they sang while they changed perches
And while they fought, if they remembered to fight:
So earnest were they to pack into that hour
Their unwilling hoard of song before the moon
Grew brighter than the clouds. Then 'twas no time
For singing merely. So they could keep off silence
And night, they cared not what they sang or screamed;
Whether 'twas hoarse or sweet or fierce or soft;

And to me all was sweet: they could do no wrong.
Something they knew – I also, while they sang
And after. Not till night had half its stars
And never a cloud, was I aware of silence
Stained with all that hour's songs, a silence
Saying that Spring returns, perhaps tomorrow.

11 march

'"Hope" is the thing with feathers'
Emily Dickinson (1830–1886)

'Hope' is the thing with feathers –
That perches in the soul –
And sings the tune without the words –
And never stops – at all –

And sweetest – in the Gale – is heard –
And sore must be the storm –
That could abash the little Bird
That kept so many warm –

I've heard it in the chillest land –
And on the strangest Sea –
Yet, never, in Extremity,
It asked a crumb – of Me.

12 march

Essay on Friendship (extract)
Mary Leapor (1722-1746)

Good breeding, wit and learning, all conspire
To charm mankind and make the world admire,
Yet in a friend but serve an under part:
The main ingredient is an honest heart.

13 march

Invictus
W. E. Henley (1849–1903)

Out of the night that covers me,
   Black as the Pit from pole to pole,
I thank whatever gods may be
   For my unconquerable soul.

In the fell clutch of circumstance
   I have not winced nor cried aloud.
Under the bludgeonings of chance
   My head is bloody, but unbowed.

Beyond this place of wrath and tears
   Looms but the Horror of the shade,
And yet the menace of the years
   Finds, and shall find, me unafraid.

It matters not how strait the gate,
   How charged with punishments the scroll,
I am the master of my fate:
   I am the captain of my soul.

14 march

'Bed is too small for my tiredness'
Anonymous

Bed is too small for my tiredness,
Give me a hilltop with trees.
Tuck a cloud up under my chin,
Lord blow the moon out, please.

Rock me to sleep in a cradle of dreams,
Send me a lullaby of leaves.
Tuck a cloud up under my chin,
Lord blow the moon out, please.

15 march

Ode to Wisdom (extract)
Elizabeth Carter (1717–1806)

The solitary bird of night
Through the pale shades now wings his flight,
   And quits the time-shook tower;
Where, sheltered from the blaze of day,
In philosophic gloom he lay,
   Beneath his bower.

With joy I hear the solemn sound,
Which midnight echoes waft around,
   And sighing gales repeat.
   Favourite of Pallas! I attend,
And, faithful to thy summons, bend
   At Wisdom's awful seat.

She loves the cool, the silent eve,
Where no false shows of life deceive,
   Beneath the lunar ray.
Here Folly drops each vain disguise,
Nor sport her gaily-coloured dyes,
   As in the beam of day.

O Pallas! queen of every art
That glads the sense, or mends the heart,
   Blest source of purer joys:
In every form of beauty bright,
That captivates the mental sight
   With pleasure and surprise:

At thy unspotted shrine I bow:
Attend thy modest suppliant's vow,
   That breathes no wild desires:
But, taught by thy unerring rules
To shun the fruitless wish of fools,
   To nobler views aspires.

From envy, hurry, noise and strife,
The dull impertinence of life,
   In thy retreat I rest:
Pursue thee to the peaceful groves,
Where Plato's sacred spirit roves,
   In all thy graces dressed.

16 march

Romeo and Juliet Act 3, Scene 2 (extract)
William Shakespeare (c. 1564–1616)

Come, night. Come, Romeo. Come, thou day in night;
For thou wilt lie upon the wings of night
Whiter than new snow on a raven's back.
Come, gentle night, come, loving, black-browed night.
Give me my Romeo. And when I shall die,
Take him and cut him out in little stars,
And he will make the face of heaven so fine
That all the world will be in love with night
And pay no worship to the garish sun.

17 march

To S.M., a Young African Painter, on Seeing His Works (extract)
Phillis Wheatley (1753–1784)

Calm and serene thy moments glide along,
And may the muse inspire each future song!
Still, with the sweets of contemplation bless'd,
May peace with balmy wings your soul invest!
But when these shades of time are chas'd away,
And darkness ends in everlasting day,
On what seraphic pinions shall we move,
And view the landscapes in the realms above?
There shall thy tongue in heav'nly murmurs flow,
And there my muse with heav'nly transport glow:
No more to tell of Damon's tender sighs,
Or rising radiance of Aurora's eyes,
For nobler themes demand a nobler strain,
And purer language on th' ethereal plain.
Cease, gentle muse! the solemn gloom of night
Now seals the fair creation from my sight.

18 march

'So, we'll go no more a roving'
George Gordon, Lord Byron (1788–1824)

So, we'll go no more a roving
   So late into the night,
Though the heart be still as loving,
   And the moon be still as bright.

For the sword outwears its sheath,
   And the soul wears out the breast,
And the heart must pause to breathe,
   And love itself have rest.

Though the night was made for loving,
   And the day returns too soon,
Yet we'll go no more a roving
   By the light of the moon.

19 march

'To every thing there is a season'
from Ecclesiastes

To every thing there is a season, and a time to every purpose under
   the heaven:
A time to be born, and a time to die; a time to plant, and a time to pluck
   up that which is planted;
A time to kill, and a time to heal; a time to break down, and a time to
   build up;
A time to weep, and a time to laugh; a time to mourn, and a time
   to dance;
A time to cast away stones, and a time to gather stones together; a time
   to embrace, and a time to refrain from embracing;
A time to get, and a time to lose; a time to keep, and a time to cast away;
A time to rend, and a time to sew; a time to keep silence, and a time
   to speak;
A time to love, and a time to hate; a time of war, and a time of peace.

20 march

Song of a Spirit (extract)
Ann Radcliffe (1764–1823)

Oft I mount with rapid force
   Above the wide earth's shadowy zone;
Follow the day-star's flaming course
   Through realms of space to thought unknown:

And listen oft celestial sounds
   That swell the air unheard of men,
As I watch my nightly rounds
O'er woody steep, and silent glen.

Under the shade of waving trees,
   On the green bank of fountain clear,
At pensive eve I sit at ease,
   While dying music murmurs near.

And oft, on point of airy clift,
   That hangs upon the western main,
I watch the gay tints passing swift,
And twilight veil the liquid plain.

21 march

Magna Est Veritas
Coventry Patmore (1823–1896)

Here, in this little Bay,
Full of tumultuous life and great repose,
Where, twice a day,
The purposeless, glad ocean comes and goes,
Under high cliffs, and far from the huge town,
I sit me down.
For want of me the world's course will not fail:
When all its work is done, the lie shall rot:
The truth is great, and shall prevail,
When none cares whether it prevail or not.

22 march

A Psalm of Life (extract)
Henry Wadsworth Longfellow (1807-1882)

Lives of great men all remind us
We can make our lives sublime,
And, departing, leave behind us
Footprints on the sands of time;

Footprints, that perhaps another,
Sailing o'er life's solemn main,
A forlorn and shipwrecked brother,
Seeing, shall take heart again.

Let us, then, be up and doing,
With a heart for any fate;
Still achieving, still pursuing,
Learn to labour and to wait.

23 march

'All day I've toiled, but not with pain'
Emily Brontë (1818-1848)

All day I've toiled, but not with pain,
In learning's golden mine;
And now at eventide again
The moonbeams softly shine.

There is no snow upon the ground,
No frost on wind or wave;
The south wind blew with gentlest sound
And broke their icy grave.

'Tis sweet to wander here at night
To watch the winter die,
With heart as summer sunshine light
And warm as summer sky.

O may I never lose the peace
That lulls me gently now,
Though time should change my youthful face,
And years should shade my brow!

True to myself, and true to all,
May I be healthful still,
And turn away from passion's call,
And curb my own wild will.

24 march

Sowing
Edward Thomas (1878–1917)

It was a perfect day
For sowing; just
As sweet and dry was the ground
As tobacco-dust.

I tasted deep the hour
Between the far
Owl's chuckling first soft cry
And the first star.

A long stretched hour it was;
Nothing undone
Remained; the early seeds
All safely sown.

And now, hark at the rain,
Windless and light,
Half a kiss, half a tear,
Saying good-night.

25 march

'Golden slumbers kiss your eyes'
Thomas Dekker (1572–1632)

Golden slumbers kiss your eyes,
Smiles awake you when you rise.
Sleep, pretty wantons, do not cry,
And I will sing a lullaby:
Rock them, rock them, lullaby.

Care is heavy, therefore sleep you;
You are care, and care must keep you.
Sleep, pretty wantons, do not cry,
And I will sing a lullaby:
Rock them, rock them, lullaby.

26 march

Courage
Amelia Earhart (1897-1939)

Courage is the price that Life exacts for granting peace.

The soul that knows it not knows no release
From little things:

Knows not the livid loneliness of fear,
Nor mountain heights where bitter joy can hear
The sound of wings.

How can life grant us boon of living, compensate
For dull gray ugliness and pregnant hate
Unless we dare

The soul's dominion? Each time we make a choice, we pay
With courage to behold the resistless day,
And count it fair.

27 march

'Care-charming sleep'
John Fletcher (1579-1625)

Care-charming Sleep, thou easer of all woes,
Brother to Death, sweetly thyself dispose
On this afflicted prince; fall like a cloud
In gentle showers; give nothing that is loud
Or painful to his slumbers; easy, sweet,
And as a purling stream, thou son of Night,
Pass by his troubled senses; sing his pain,
Like hollow murmuring wind or silver rain;
Into this prince gently, oh gently slide,
And kiss him into slumbers like a bride.

28 march

Moonlight and Gas
Constance Naden (1858–1889)

The poet in theory worships the moon,
   But how can he linger, to gaze on her light?
With proof-sheets and copy the table is strewn,
   A poem lies there, to be finished to-night.
He silently watches the queen of the sky,
   But orbs more prosaic must dawn for him soon –
The gas must be lighted; he turns with a sigh,
   Lets down his venetians and shuts out the moon.

'This is but symbol,' he sadly exclaims,
   'Heaven's glory must yield to the lustre of earth;
More golden, less distant, less pure are the flames
   That shine for the world over sorrow and mirth.
When Wisdom sublime sheds her beams o'er the night,
   I turn with a sigh from the coveted boon,
And choosing instead a more practical light
   Let down my venetians and shut out the moon.'

He sits to his desk and he mutters 'Alas,
   My muse will not waken, and yet I must write!'
But great is Diana: venetians and gas
   Have not been sufficient to banish her quite.
She peeps through the blinds and is bright as before,
   He smiles and he blesses the hint opportune,
And feels he can still, when his labour is o'er,
   Draw up his venetians and welcome the moon.

29 march

Prayer (I)
George Herbert (1593–1633)

Prayer, the Church's banquet, Angels' age,
    God's breath in man returning to his birth,
    The soul in paraphrase, heart in pilgrimage,
The Christian plummet sounding heav'n and earth;
Engine against th'Almighty, sinners' tower,
    Reversed thunder, Christ-side-piercing spear,
    The six-days world-transposing in an hour,
A kind of tune, which all things hear and fear;
Softness, and peace, and joy, and love, and bliss,
    Exalted Manna, gladness of the best,
    Heaven in ordinary, man well dressed,
The milky way, the bird of Paradise,
    Church-bells beyond the stars heard, the soul's blood,
    The land of spices; something understood.

30 march

Tell Good People Good Things
Salena Godden (b. 1972)

Tell each other you love each other.
Say love. Show your love. Speak it.

Do not wait to talk to a flower
in the hope the dead will hear the love
you could've said before.

Do not wait to talk to headstones
And weep at faded photographs.

Please do not die with all unsaid
and then haunt your loved ones
appearing in night and shadow and dream.

You are alive now. So love now.

Tell your good people all the good things.
Tell each other you love each other.

Do not wait to softly weep to flickering candles
or cry about your love to a flower too late.

Say love. Show your love. Share it.

31 march

Hymn to Diana
Ben Jonson (1572-1637)

Queen and Huntress, chaste and fair,
Now the sun is laid to sleep,
Seated in thy silver chair
State in wonted manner keep:
Hesperus entreats thy light,
Goddess excellently bright.

Earth, let not thy envious shade
Dare itself to interpose;
Cynthia's shining orb was made
Heaven to clear when day did close:
Bless us then with wishèd sight,
Goddess excellently bright.

Lay thy bow of pearl apart
And thy crystal-shining quiver;
Give unto the flying hart
Space to breath, how short soever;
Thou that mak'st a day of night,
Goddess excellently bright.

april

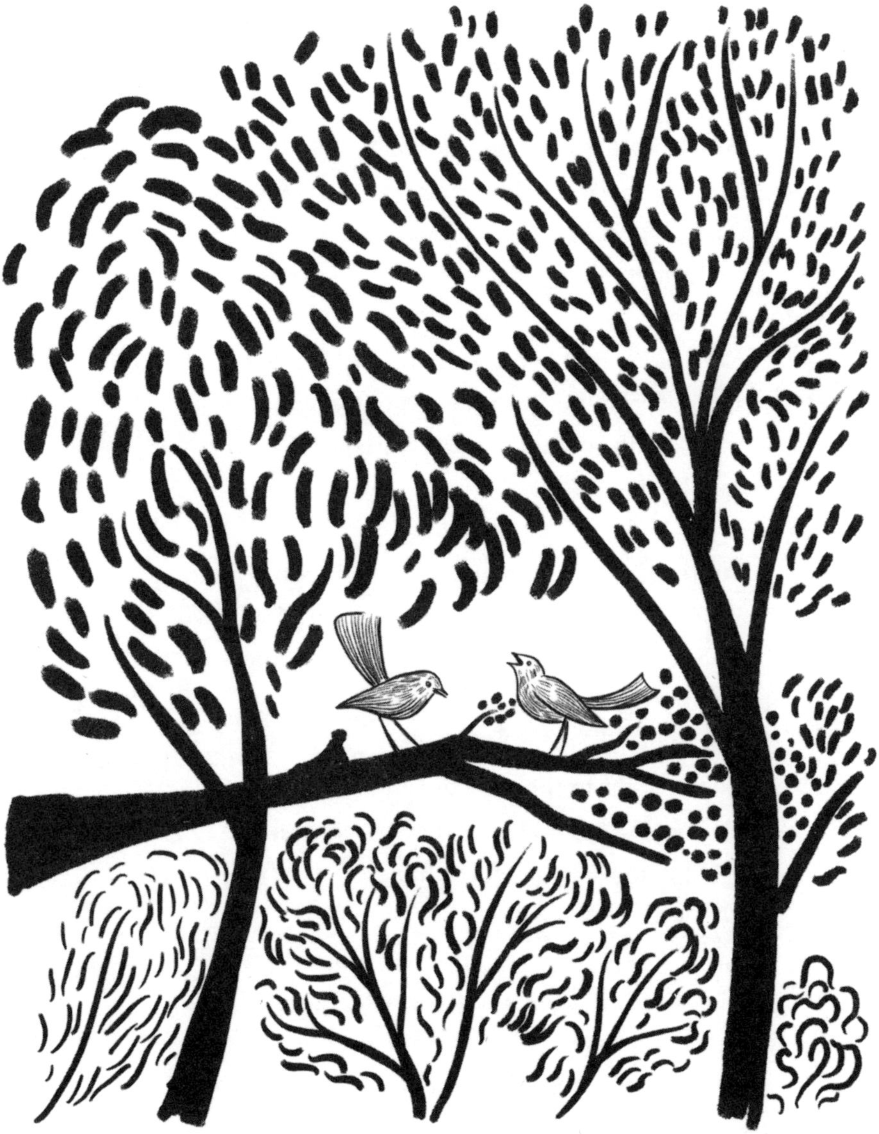

1 april

Night
Sidney Lanier (1842-1881)

A pale enchanted moon is sinking low
Behind the dunes that fringe the shadowy lea,
And there is haunted starlight on the flow
Of immemorial sea.

I am alone and need no more pretend
Laughter or smile to hide a hungry heart;
I walk with solitude as with a friend
Enfolded and apart.

We tread an eerie road across the moor
Where shadows weave upon their ghostly looms,
And winds sing an old lyric that might lure
Sad queens from ancient tombs.

I am a sister to the loveliness
Of cool far hill and long-remembered shore,
Finding in it a sweet forgetfulness
Of all that hurt before.

The world of day, its bitterness and cark,
No longer have the power to make me weep;
I welcome this communion of the dark
As toilers welcome sleep.

2 april

'I think I'd like you better, Star'
Annette Wynne (active 1919-1922)

I think I'd like you better, Star,
If you were not so high and far.
So many friendly things are found
Quite near the ground.
I wonder if I saw you near
Would you appear
So very fine; I hope you would
Be just as pretty, bright, and good –
Not like some that only are
Fine and true when seen from far.

I have little candle light,
Friendly, simple, good and bright –
I love it for it shines at night
Upon the stairs
And waits, still shining, till my prayers
Are said
And I'm about to jump to bed;
I say, 'Good-night, Dear candle light.'

I think I'd like you better, Star,
If you were only not so far.

3 april

In Sleep
Richard Francis Burton (1821–1890)

Not drowsihood and dreams and mere idles,
Nor yet the blessedness of strength regained,
Alone are in what men call sleep. The past,
My unsuspected soul, my parents' voice,
The generations of my forbears, yea,
The very will of God himself are there
And potent-working; so that many a doubt
Is wiped away at daylight, many a soil
Washed cleanlier, many a puzzle riddled plain.
Strong, silent forces push my puny self
Towards unguessed issues, and the waking man
Rises a Greatheart where a Slave lay down.

4 april

A Blessing
James Wright (1927-1980)

Just off the highway to Rochester, Minnesota,
Twilight bounds softly forth on the grass.
And the eyes of those two Indian ponies
Darken with kindness.
They have come gladly out of the willows
To welcome my friend and me.
We step over the barbed wire into the pasture
Where they have been grazing all day, alone.
They ripple tensely, they can hardly contain their happiness
That we have come.
They bow shyly as wet swans. They love each other.
There is no loneliness like theirs.
At home once more,
They begin munching the young tufts of spring in the darkness.
I would like to hold the slenderer one in my arms,
For she has walked over to me
And nuzzled my left hand.
She is black and white,
Her mane falls wild on her forehead,
And the light breeze moves me to caress her long ear
That is delicate as the skin over a girl's wrist.
Suddenly I realize
That if I stepped out of my body I would break
Into blossom.

5 *april*

The Loom of Time
Anonymous

Man's life is laid in the loom of time
    To a pattern he does not see,
While the weavers work and the shuttles fly
    Till the dawn of eternity.

Some shuttles are filled with silver threads
    And some with threads of gold,
While often but the darker hues
    Are all that they may hold.

But the weaver watches with skilful eye
    Each shuttle fly to and fro,
And sees the pattern so deftly wrought
    As the loom moves sure and slow.

God surely planned the pattern:
    Each thread, the dark and fair,
Is chosen by His master skill
    And placed in the web with care.

He only knows its beauty,
    And guides the shuttles which hold
The threads so unattractive,
    As well as the threads of gold.

Not till each loom is silent,
    And the shuttles cease to fly,
Shall God reveal the pattern
    And explain the reason why

The dark threads were as needful
    In the weaver's skilful hand
As the threads of gold and silver
    For the pattern which He planned.

6 april

Don't Quit
John Greenleaf Whittier (1807–1892)

When things go wrong as they sometimes will,
When the road you're trudging seems all uphill,
When the funds are low and the debts are high
And you want to smile, but you have to sigh,
When care is pressing you down a bit,
Rest, if you must, but don't you quit.

Life is queer with its twists and turns,
As everyone of us sometimes learns,
And many a failure turns about
When he might have won had he stuck it out,
Don't give up though the pace seems slow –
You may succeed with another blow.

Success is failure turned inside out –
The silver tint of the clouds of doubt,
And you never can tell how close you are,
It may be near when it seems so far,
So stick to the fight when you're hardest hit –
It's when things seem worst that you must not quit.

For all the sad words of tongue or pen,
The saddest are these: 'It might have been!'

7 *april*

Forgetfulness
Hart Crane (1899–1932)

Forgetfulness is like a song
That, freed from beat and measure, wanders.
Forgetfulness is like a bird whose wings are reconciled,
Outspread and motionless, –
A bird that coasts the wind unwearyingly.

Forgetfulness is rain at night,
Or an old house in a forest, – or a child.
Forgetfulness is white, – white as a blasted tree,
And it may stun the sybil into prophecy,
Or bury the Gods.

I can remember much forgetfulness.

8 april

In the Fields
Charlotte Mew (1869-1928)

Lord, when I look at lovely things which pass,
  Under old trees the shadow of young leaves
Dancing to please the wind along the grass,
  Or the gold stillness of the August sun on the August sheaves;
Can I believe there is a heavenlier world than this?
  And if there is
Will the strange heart of any everlasting thing
  Bring me these dreams that take my breath away?
They come at evening with the home-flying rooks and
    the scent of hay,
  Over the fields. They come in Spring.

9 april

Paris
Willa Cather (1873-1947)

Behind the arch of glory sets the day;
The river lies in curves of silver light,
The Fields Elysian glitter in a spray
Of golden dust; the gilded dome is bright,
The towers of Notre Dame cut clean and gray
The evening sky, and pale from left to right
A hundred bridges leap from either quay.
Pillared with pride, the city of delight
Sits like an empress by her silver Seine,
Heavy with jewels, all her splendid dower
Flashing upon her, won from shore and main
By shock of combat, sacked from town and tower.
Wherever men have builded hall or fane
Red war hath gleaned for her and men have slain
To deck her loveliness. I feel again
That joy which brings her art to faultless flower,
That passion of her kings, who, reign on reign,
Arrayed her star by star with pride and power.

10 april

'The same stream of life'
Rabindranath Tagore (1861–1941)

The same stream of life that runs through my veins night and day runs through the world and dances in rhythmic measures.

It is the same life that shoots in joy through the dust of the earth in numberless blades of grass and breaks into tumultuous waves of leaves and flowers.

It is the same life that is rocked in the ocean-cradle of birth and of death, in ebb and in flow.

I feel my limbs are made glorious by the touch of this world of life. And my pride is from the life-throb of ages dancing in my blood this moment.

11 april

Planet Earth
P. K. Page (1916-2010)

It has to be spread out, the skin of this planet, has to be ironed, the sea in its whiteness, and the hands keep on moving, smoothing the holy surfaces.
— PABLO NERUDA, 'In Praise of Ironing'

It has to be loved the way a laundress loves her linens,
the way she moves her hands caressing the fine muslins
knowing their warp and woof,
like a lover coaxing, or a mother praising.
It has to be loved as if it were embroidered
with flowers and birds and two joined hearts upon it.
It has to be stretched and stroked.
It has to be celebrated.
O this great beloved world and all the creatures in it.
It has to be spread out, the skin of this planet.

The trees must be washed, and the grasses and mosses.
They have to be polished as if made of green brass.
The rivers and little streams with their hidden cresses
and pale-coloured pebbles
and their fool's gold
must be washed and starched or shined into brightness,
the sheets of lake water
smoothed with the hand
and the foam of the oceans pressed into neatness.
It has to be ironed, the sea in its whiteness

[cont.]

and pleated and goffered, the flower-blue sea
the protean, wine-dark, grey, green, sea
with its metres of satin and bolts of brocade.
And sky – such an O! overhead – night and day
must be burnished and rubbed
by hands that are loving
so the blue blazons forth
and the stars keep on shining
within and above
and the hands keep on moving.

It has to be made bright, the skin of this planet
till it shines in the sun like gold leaf.
Archangels then will attend to its metals
and polish the rods of its rain.
Seraphim will stop singing hosannas
to shower it with blessings and blisses and praises,
and, newly in love,
we must draw it and paint it
our pencils and brushes and loving caresses
smoothing the holy surfaces.

12 april

Paradise Lost (extract)
John Milton (1608-1674)

Sweet is the breath of Morn; her rising sweet,
With charm of earliest birds: pleasant the sun,
When first on this delightful land he spreads
His orient beams, on herb, tree, fruit, and flower,
Glistering with dew; fragrant the fertile earth
After soft showers; and sweet the coming on
Of grateful Evening mild; then silent Night,
With this her solemn bird, and this fair moon,
And these the gems of Heaven, her starry train.

13 april

'What are heavy?'
Christina Rossetti (1830–1894)

What are heavy? Sea-sand and sorrow:
What are brief? To-day and to-morrow:
What are frail? Spring blossoms and youth:
What are deep? The ocean and truth.

14 april

A Song in the Night
George MacDonald (1824–1905)

A brown bird sang on a blossomy tree,
Sang in the moonshine, merrily,
Three little songs, one, two, and three,
A song for his wife, for himself, and me.

He sang for his wife, sang low, sang high,
Filling the moonlight that filled the sky;
'Thee, thee, I love thee, heart alive!
Thee, thee, thee, and thy round eggs five!'

He sang to himself, 'What shall I do
With this life that thrills me through and through!
Glad is so glad that it turns to ache!
Out with it, song, or my heart will break!'

He sang to me, 'Man, do not fear
Though the moon goes down and the dark is near;
Listen my song and rest thine eyes;
Let the moon go down that the sun may rise!'

I folded me up in the heart of his tune,
And fell asleep with the sinking moon;
I woke with the day's first golden gleam,
And, lo, I had dreamed a precious dream!

15 april

A Scherzo (a Shy Person's Wishes)
Dora Greenwell (1821–1882)

With the wasp at the innermost heart of a peach,
On a sunny wall out of tip-toe reach,
With the trout in the darkest summer pool,
With the fern-seed clinging behind its cool
Smooth frond, in the chink of an aged tree,
In the woodbine's horn with the drunken bee,
With the mouse in its nest in a furrow old,
With the chrysalis wrapt in its gauzy fold;
With things that are hidden, and safe, and bold,
With things that are timid, and shy, and free,
Wishing to be;
With the nut in its shell, with the seed in its pod,
With the corn as it sprouts in the kindly clod,
Far down where the secret of beauty shows
In the bulb of the tulip, before it blows;
With things that are rooted, and firm, and deep,
Quiet to lie, and dreamless to sleep;
With things that are chainless, and tameless, and proud,
With the fire in the jagged thunder-cloud,
With the wind in its sleep, with the wind in its waking,
With the drops that go to the rainbow's making,
Wishing to be with the light leaves shaking,
The dew as it falls, or the dust as it rises;

Or stones on some desolate highway breaking;
Far up on the hills, where no foot surprises
The dew as it falls, or the dust as it rises;
To be couched with the beast in its torrid lair,
Or drifting on ice with the polar bear,
With the weaver at work at his quiet loom;
Anywhere, anywhere, out of this room!

16 april

'In the evening'
Fenton Johnson (1888-1958)

In the evening, love returns,
   Like a wand'rer 'cross the sea;
In the evening, love returns
   With a violet for me;
In the evening, life's a song,
   And the fields are full of green;
All the stars are golden crowns,
   And the eye of God is keen.

In the evening, sorrow dies
   With the setting of the sun;
In the evening, joy begins,
   When the course of mirth is done;
In the evening, kisses sweet
   Droop upon the passion vine;
In the evening comes your voice:
   'I am yours, and you are mine.'

17 april

'Say not the struggle nought availeth'
Arthur Hugh Clough (1819–1861)

Say not the struggle nought availeth,
  The labour and the wounds are vain,
The enemy faints not, nor faileth,
  And as things have been, things remain.

If hopes were dupes, fears may be liars;
  It may be, in yon smoke concealed,
Your comrades chase e'en now the fliers,
  And, but for you, possess the field.

For while the tired waves, vainly breaking,
  Seem here no painful inch to gain,
Far back through creeks and inlets making
  Came, silent, flooding in, the main,

And not by eastern windows only,
  When daylight comes, comes in the light,
In front the sun climbs slow, how slowly,
  But westward, look, the land is bright.

18 april

'There will come soft rains'
Sara Teasdale (1884-1933)

There will come soft rains and the smell of the ground,
And swallows circling with their shimmering sound;

And frogs in the pools, singing at night,
And wild plum trees in tremulous white,

Robins will wear their feathery fire,
Whistling their whims on a low fence-wire;

And not one will know of the war, not one
Will care at last when it is done.

Not one would mind, neither bird nor tree,
If mankind perished utterly;

And Spring herself, when she woke at dawn,
Would scarcely know that we were gone.

19 april

Ode on a Distant Prospect of Eton College (extract)
Thomas Gray (1716-1771)

Ye distant spires, ye antique towers,
   That crown the watery glade,
Where grateful Science still adores
   Her Henry's holy shade;
And ye, that from the stately brow
Of Windsor's heights the expanse below
   Of grove, of lawn, of mead survey,
Whose turf, whose shade, whose flowers among
Wanders the hoary Thames along
   His silver-winding way.

Ah, happy hills, ah, pleasing shade,
   Ah, fields beloved in vain,
Where once my careless childhood strayed,
   A stranger yet to pain!
I feel the gales, that from ye blow,
A momentary bliss bestow,
   As waving fresh their gladsome wing,
My weary soul they seem to soothe,
And, redolent of joy and youth,
   To breathe a second spring.

20 april

The Washing
Jaan Kaplinski (1941-2021)

The washing never gets done.
The furnace never gets heated.
Books never get read.
Life is never completed.
Life is like a ball which one must continually
catch and hit so it won't fall.
When the fence is repaired at one end,
it collapses on the other. The roof leaks,
the kitchen door won't close, there are cracks in the foundation,
the torn knees of children's pants . . .
One can't keep everything in mind. The wonder is
that beside all this one can notice
the spring which is so full of everything
continuing in all directions – into the evening clouds,
into the redwing's song and into every
drop of dew on every blade of grass in the meadow,
as far as the eye can see, into the dusk.

21 april

Endymion (extract)
John Keats (1795–1821)

A thing of beauty is a joy for ever:
Its loveliness increases; it will never
Pass into nothingness; but still will keep
A bower quiet for us, and a sleep
Full of sweet dreams, and health, and quiet breathing.
Therefore, on every morrow, are we wreathing
A flowery band to bind us to the earth,
Spite of despondence, of the inhuman dearth
Of noble natures, of the gloomy days,
Of all the unhealthy and o'er-darkened ways
Made for our searching: yes, in spite of all,
Some shape of beauty moves away the pall
From our dark spirits. Such the sun, the moon,
Trees old and young, sprouting a shady boon
For simple sheep; and such are daffodils
With the green world they live in; and clear rills
That for themselves a cooling covert make
'Gainst the hot season; the mid-forest brake,
Rich with a sprinkling of fair musk-rose blooms:
And such too is the grandeur of the dooms
We have imagined for the mighty dead;
All lovely tales that we have heard or read:
An endless fountain of immortal drink,
Pouring unto us from the heaven's brink.

22 april

To Sleep
Maybury Fleming (1853–c.1929)

Sweet wooded way in life, forgetful Sleep!
Dim, drowsy realm where restful shadows fall,
And where the world's glare enters not at all,
Or in soft glimmer making rest more deep;
Where sound comes not, or else like brooks that keep
The world's noise out, as by a slumberous wall

Of gentlest murmur, where still whispers call
To smileless gladness those that waking weep;
Beneath the dense veil of thy stirless leaves,
Where no air is except the calm of space,
Vexed souls of men have grateful widow-hood
Of tedious sense; there thoughts are bound in sheaves
By viewless hands as silent as the place;
And man, unsinning, finds all nature good.

23 april

The Tempest Act 4, Scene 1 (extract)
William Shakespeare (c. 1564–1616)

Our revels now are ended. These our actors,
As I foretold you, were all spirits, and
Are melted into air, into thin air;
And, like the baseless fabric of this vision,
The cloud-capped towers, the gorgeous palaces,
The solemn temples, the great globe itself,
Yea, all which it inherit, shall dissolve,
And like this insubstantial pageant faded,
Leave not a rack behind. We are such stuff
As dreams are made on, and our little life
Is rounded with a sleep.

24 april

Scenes from Life on Earth
Kathryn Simmonds (b. 1972)

I loved the trees,
I didn't learn their names
but muddled them
into one gorgeous lanky family;

I loved their cool, slim hips
their sudden splits
their tender dark
their never ending want for sky;

I loved their interlaced attentiveness
their flair for being still
or keeping time with any
off-beat breeze.

I loved the trees because
they had redemption down,
oh God be glorified, I loved the trees!
The way they ate their old regrets
              and made them into leaves.

25 april

'If all were rain and never sun'
Christina Rossetti (1830–1894)

If all were rain and never sun,
No bow could span the hill;
If all were sun and never rain,
There'd be no rainbow still.

26 april

Bells in the Rain (extract)
Elinor Wylie (1885–1928)

Sleep falls, with limpid drops of rain,
Upon the steep cliffs of the town.
Sleep falls; men are at peace again
While the small drops fall softly down.

The bright drops ring like bells of glass
Thinned by the wind, and lightly blown;
Sleep cannot fall on peaceful grass
So softly as it falls on stone.

27 april

Night
William Blake (1757–1827)

The sun descending in the west.
The evening star does shine.
The birds are silent in their nest,
And I must seek for mine,
The moon like a flower,
In heaven's high bower;
With silent delight,
Sits and smiles on the night.

Farewell green fields and happy groves,
Where flocks have took delight;
Where lambs have nibbled, silent moves
The feet of angels bright;
Unseen they pour blessing,
And joy without ceasing,
On each bud and blossom,
And each sleeping bosom.

They look in every thoughtless nest
Where birds are cover'd warm;
They visit caves of every beast,
To keep them all from harm;
If they see any weeping,
That should have been sleeping
They pour sleep on their head
And sit down by their bed.

[cont.]

When wolves and tygers howl for prey
They pitying stand and weep;
Seeking to drive their thirst away,
And keep them from the sheep.
But if they rush dreadful;
The angels most heedful,
Receive each mild spirit.
New worlds to inherit.

And there the lion's ruddy eyes,
Shall flow with tears of gold;
And pitying the tender cries,
And walking round the fold:
Saying: wrath by his meekness
And by his health, sickness,
Is driven away,
From our immortal day.

And now beside thee, bleating lamb.
I can lie down and sleep;
Or think on him who bore thy name.
Grase after thee and weep.
For wash'd in life's river.
My bright mane for ever.
Shall shine like the gold.
As I guard o'er the fold.

28 april

Woods: A Prose Sonnet
Ralph Waldo Emerson (1803–1882)

Wise are ye, O ancient woods! Wiser than man. Whoso goeth in your paths or into your thickets where no paths are, readeth the same cheerful lesson whether he be a young child or a hundred years old. Comes he in good fortune or bad, ye say the same things, & from age to age. Ever the needles of the pine grow & fall, the acorns on the oak, the maples redden in autumn, & at all times of the year the ground pine & the pyrola bud & root under foot. What is called fortune & what is called Time by men – ye know them not. Men have not language to describe one moment of your eternal life. This I would ask of you, O, sacred Woods, when ye shall next give me somewhat to say, give me also the tune wherein to say it. Give me a tune of your own like your winds or rains or brooks or birds; for the songs of men grow old when they have been often repeated, but yours, though a man have heard them for seventy years, are never the same, but always new, like time itself, or like love.

29 april

My Voysey Wall-Paper
Margaret Armour (1860-1943)

I have two gardens for my ease,
Where skies are warm and flowers please;
With skilful mastery each designed
Is fair and perfect of its kind.
In one the tulips every year
Flame April out and disappear;
And roses red that garland June
Are worn but for a summer's noon.
It is a garden, flower and leaf,
Where lovely things are very brief.

Upon a wall my other grows,
And changes not for heat or snows.
Its tulips do not flaunt and die,
But, dreaming, watch the spring go by.
In pensive grey, like musing nuns,
They hold no commerce with the suns.
There leaves in order are outspread
Which ruffling winds shall never shed.
The roses are the magic blue
That in the faery gardens grew,
Not fashioned for themselves alone,
But for the common beauty grown.

They shall not wax, they shall not wane,
They shall not flush to fleet again,
But quaintly, in their quiet place,
Shall charm me with unaltered grace,
And fresh for ever, flower and shoot,
Shall spring from their eternal root.

30 april

He Wishes for the Cloths of Heaven
W. B. Yeats (1865-1939)

Had I the heavens' embroidered cloths,
Enwrought with golden and silver light,
The blue and the dim and the dark cloths
Of night and light and the half-light,
I would spread the cloths under your feet:
But I, being poor, have only my dreams;
I have spread my dreams under your feet;
Tread softly because you tread on my dreams.

may

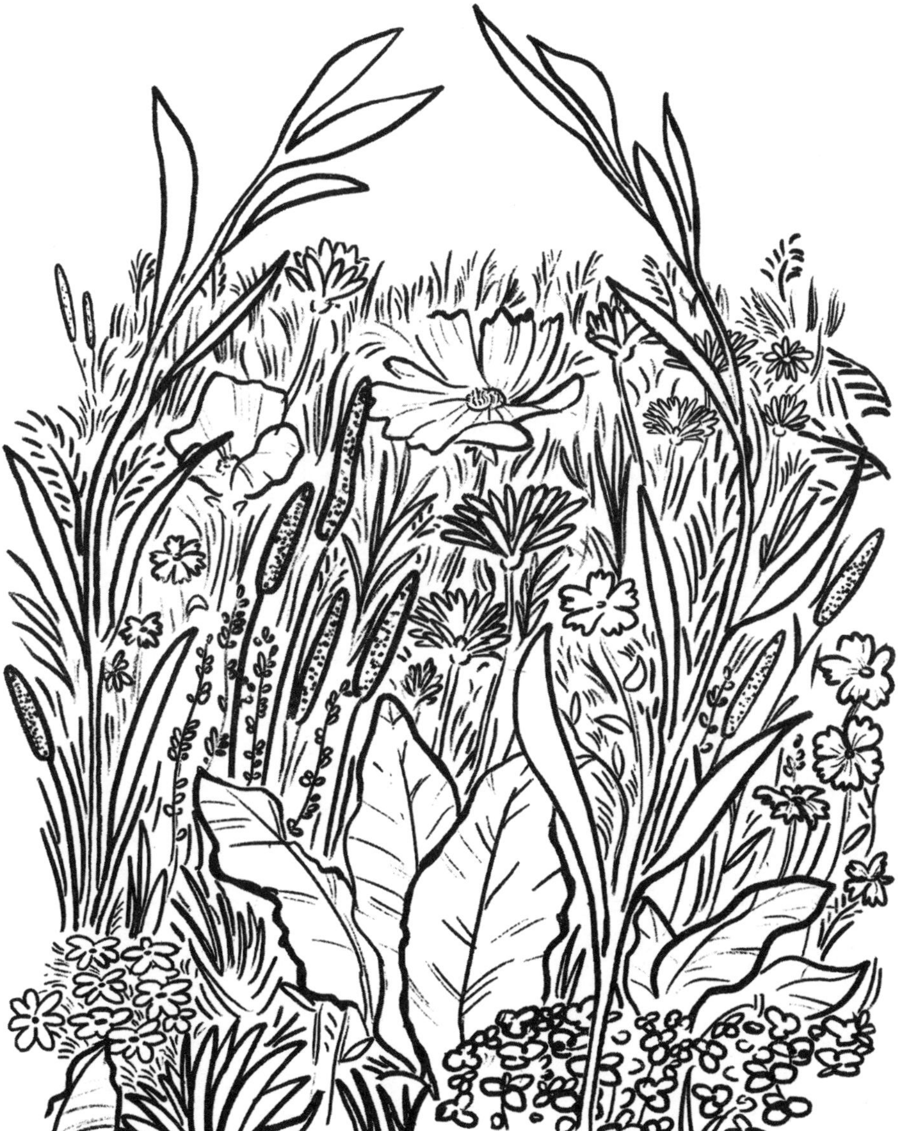

1 may

'All nature has a feeling'
John Clare (1793-1864)

All nature has a feeling: woods, brooks, fields
Are life eternal – and in silence they
Speak happiness – beyond the reach of books;
There's nothing mortal in them – their decay
Is the green life of change; to pass away
And come again in blooms revivified
Its birth was heaven eternal is its stay
And with the sun and moon shall still abide
Beneath their night and day and heaven wide

2 may

The Happy Heart
Thomas Dekker (1572-1632)

Art thou poor, yet hast thou golden slumbers?
   O sweet content!
Art thou rich, yet is thy mind perplexéd?
   O punishment!
Dost thou laugh to see how fools are vexéd
To add to golden numbers, golden numbers?
O sweet content! O sweet, O sweet content!
     Work apace, apace, apace, apace;
     Honest labour bears a lovely face;
Then hey nonny nonny, hey nonny nonny!

Canst drink the waters of the crispéd spring?
   O sweet content!
Swimm'st thou in wealth, yet sink'st in thine own tears?
   O punishment!
Then he that patiently want's burden bears
No burden bears, but is a king, a king!
O sweet content! O sweet, O sweet content!
     Work apace, apace, apace, apace;
     Honest labour bears a lovely face;
Then hey nonny nonny, hey nonny nonny!

3 may

'Twilight and I went hand in hand'
Lucy Maud Montgomery (1874–1942)

Twilight and I went hand in hand,
As lovers walk in shining Mays,
O'er musky, memory-haunted ways,
Across a lonely harvest-land,
Where west winds chanted in the wheat
An old, old vesper wondrous sweet.

Oh, Twilight was a comrade rare
For gypsy heath or templed grove,
In her gray vesture, shadow-wove;
I saw the darkness of her hair
Faint-mirrored in a field-pool dim,
As we stood tip-toe on its rim.

We went as lightly as on wings
Through many a scented chamber fair,
Among the pines and balsams, where
I could have dreamed of darling things,
And ever as we went I knew
The peeping fairy folk went too.

I could have lingered now and then
By gates of moonrise that might lead
To some forgotten, spiceried mead,
Or in some mossy, cloistered glen,
Where silence, very still and deep,
Seemed fallen in enchanted sleep.

But Twilight ever led me on,
As lovers walk, until we came
To hills where sunset's shaken flame
Had paled to ashes dead and wan;
And there, with footsteps stolen-light
She left me to the lure of night.

4 may

May, 1915
Charlotte Mew *(1869-1928)*

      Let us remember Spring will come again
To the scorched blackened woods where all the wounded trees
   Wait, with the old wise patience for the heavenly rain,
Sure of the sky, sure of the sea to send its healing breeze,
      Sure of the sun. And even as to these
      Surely the Spring, when God shall please,
   Will come again like a divine surprise
To those who sit to-day with their Great Dead, hands in their
   hands, eyes in their eyes,
At one with Love, at one with Grief, blind to the scattered things
   and changing skies.

5 may

In the Forest
Oscar Wilde (1854–1900)

Out of the mid-wood's twilight
   Into the meadow's dawn,
Ivory-limbed and brown-eyed,
   Flashes my Faun!

He skips through the copses singing,
   And his shadow dances along,
And I know not which I should follow,
   Shadow or song!

O Hunter, snare me his shadow!
   O Nightingale, catch me his strain!
Else moonstruck with music and madness
   I track him in vain!

6 *may*

An Evening Prospect (extract)
Ann Eliza Bleecker (1752–1783)

Come, my Susan, quit your chamber,
   Greet the opening bloom of May,
Let us up yon hillock clamber,
   And around the scene survey.

See the sun is now descending,
   And projects his shadows far,
And the bee her course is bending
   Homeward through the humid air.

Mark the lizard just before us,
   Singing her unvaried strain,
While the frog abrupt in chorus
   Deepens through the marshy plain.

From yon grove the woodcock rises,
   Mark her progress by her notes,
High in air her wing she poises,
   Then like lightning down she shoots.

Now the whip-poor-will beginning,
   Clamorous on a pointed rail,
Drowns the more melodious singing
   Of the catbird, thrush, and quail.

Pensive Echo from the mountain
  Still repeats the sylvan sounds;
And the crocus-bordered fountain
  With the splendid fly abounds.

There the honey-suckle blooming,
  Reddens the capricious wave;
Richer sweets, the air perfuming,
  Spicy Ceylon never gave.

Cast your eyes beyond this meadow,
  Painted by a hand divine,
And observe the ample shadow
  Of that solemn ridge of pine.

Here a trickling rill depending,
  Glitters through the artless bower
And the silver dew descending,
  Doubly radiates every flower.

While I speak, the sun is vanish'd,
  All the gilded clouds are fled;
Music from the groves is banish'd,
  Noxious vapours round us spread.

Rural toil is now suspended,
  Sleep invades the peasant's eyes;
Each diurnal task is ended,
  While soft Luna climbs the skies.

7 may

Leisure
W. H. Davies (1871–1940)

What is this life if, full of care,
We have no time to stand and stare? –

No time to stand beneath the boughs,
And stare as long as sheep or cows:

No time to see, when woods we pass,
Where squirrels hide their nuts in grass:

No time to see, in broad daylight,
Streams full of stars, like skies at night:

No time to turn at Beauty's glance,
And watch her feet, how they can dance:

No time to wait till her mouth can
Enrich that smile her eyes began?

A poor life this if, full of care,
We have no time to stand and stare.

8 may

'If you look for the truth outside yourself'
Tung-Shan (c. 807–869)

If you look for the truth outside yourself,
it gets farther and farther away.
Today, walking alone,
I meet him everywhere I step.
He is the same as me,
yet, I am not him.
Only if you understand it in this way
will you merge with the way things are.

9 *may*

The Old Love
Katharine Tynan (1859–1931)

Out of my door I step into
The country; all her scent and dew,
Nor travel there by a hard road,
Dusty and far from my abode.

The country washes to my door
Green miles on miles in soft uproar,
The thunder of the woods, and then
The backwash of green surf again.

Beyond the feverfew and stocks,
The guelder-rose and hollyhocks;
Outside my trellised porch a tree
Of lilac frames a sky for me.

A stretch of primrose and pale green
To hold the tender Hesper in;
Hesper that by the moon makes pale
Her silver keel and silver sail.

The country silence wraps me quite,
Silence and song and pure delight;
The country beckons all the day
Smiling, and but a step away.

This is that country seen across
How many a league of love and loss,
Prayed for and longed for; and as far
As fountains in the desert are.

This is that country at my door,
Whose fragrant airs run on before,
And call me when the first birds stir
In the green wood to walk with her.

10 may

To the Nightingale
John Donne (1572–1631)

Sweet bird, that sing'st away the early hours
Of winters past or coming, void of care,
Well pleased with delights which present are,
(Fair seasons, budding sprays, sweet-smelling flowers)
To rocks, to springs, to rills, from leafy bowers
Thou thy Creator's goodness dost declare,
And what dear gifts on thee He did not spare:
A stain to human sense in sin that lours,
What soul can be so sick which by thy songs
(Attired in sweetness) sweetly is not driven
Quite to forget earth's turmoils, spites, and wrongs,
And lift a reverend eye and thought to heaven?
Sweet artless songster, thou my mind dost raise
To airs of spheres, yes, and to angels' lays.

11 may

Nightingale
Christian Carstairs (1763–1786)

O! Could my sweet plaint lull to rest,
Soften one sigh – as thou dreamst,
I'd sit the whole night on thy tree,
And sing, – – sing, – –
   With the thorn at my breast.

12 may

The Nightingale Near the House
Harold Monro (1879–1932)

Here is the soundless cypress on the lawn:
It listens, listens. Taller trees beyond
Listen. The moon at the unruffled pond
   Stares. And you sing, you sing.

  That star-enchanted song falls through the air
From lawn to lawn down terraces of sound,
Darts in white arrows on the shadowed grounds;
   While all the night you sing.

  My dreams are flowers to which you are a bee,
As all night long I listen, and my brain
Receives your song, then loses it again
   In moonlight on the lawn.

  Now is your voice a marble high and white,
Then like a mist on fields of paradise;
Now is a raging fire, then is like ice,
   Then breaks, and it is dawn.

13 may

Good-night
Edward Thomas (1878–1917)

The skylarks are far behind that sang over the down;
I can hear no more those suburb nightingales;
Thrushes and blackbirds sing in the gardens of the town
In vain: the noise of man, beast, and machine prevails.

But the call of children in the unfamiliar streets
That echo with a familiar twilight echoing,
Sweet as the voice of nightingale or lark, completes
A magic of strange welcome, so that I seem a king

Among man, beast, machine, bird, child, and the ghost
That in the echo lives and with the echo dies.
The friendless town is friendly; homeless, I not lost;
Though I know none of these doors, and meet but strangers' eyes.

Never again, perhaps, after tomorrow, shall
I see these homely streets, these church windows alight,
Not a man or woman or child among them all:
But it is All Friends' Night, a traveller's good night.

14 may

Departed Youth
Hannah Cowley (1743-1809)

What though the rosebuds from my cheek
Have faded all! which once so sleek
Spoke youth, and joy, and careless thought.
By guilt, or fear, or shame uncaught,
My soul, uninjured, still hath youth,
Its lively sense attests the truth!
   Oh! I can wander yet, and taste
The beauties of the flowery waste,
The nightingale's deep swell can feel
Till to the eye a tear doth steal;
Rapt! gaze upon the gem-decked night,
Or mark the clear moon's gradual flight,
Whilst the bright river's rippled wave
Repeats the quivering beams she gave.
   Nor yet does Painting strive in vain
To waken from its canvas plain
The lofty passions of the mind,
Or hint the sentiment refined:
To the sweet magic yet I bow,
As when youth decked my polished brow.
The chisel's lightest touch to trace
Through the pure form, or softened grace,
Is lent me still; I still admire,
And kindle at the Poet's fire –
   Why Time! since these are left me still,
Of lesser thefts e'en take thy fill.

Yes, take all lustre from my eye,
And let the blithe carnation fly,
My tresses sprinkle o'er with snow,
That boasted once their auburn glow,
Break the slim form that was adored
By him so loved, my wedded lord;
But leave me, whilst all these you steal,
The mind to taste, the nerve to feel!

15 may

The Star
Jane Taylor (1783-1824)

Twinkle, twinkle, little star,
How I wonder what you are!
Up above the world so high,
Like a diamond in the sky.

When the blazing sun is gone,
When he nothing shines upon,
Then you show your little light,
Twinkle, twinkle, all the night.

Then the traveller in the dark,
Thanks you for your tiny spark,
He could not see which way to go,
If you did not twinkle so.

In the dark blue sky you keep,
And often through my curtains peep,
For you never shut your eye,
Till the sun is in the sky.

As your bright and tiny spark,
Lights the traveller in the dark,
Though I know not what you are,
Twinkle, twinkle, little star.

16 may

Henry VIII Act 3, Scene 1 (extract)
William Shakespeare (c. 1564–1616)

Orpheus with his lute made trees,
And the mountain tops that freeze,
Bow themselves when he did sing.
To his music plants and flowers
Ever sprung, as sun and showers
There had made a lasting spring.

Everything that heard him play,
Even the billows of the sea,
Hung their heads, and then lay by.
In sweet music is such art,
Killing care and grief of heart
Fall asleep, or hearing die.

17 may

So Much Happiness
Naomi Shihab Nye (b. 1952)

It is difficult to know what to do with so much happiness.
With sadness there is something to rub against,
a wound to tend with lotion and cloth.
When the world falls in around you, you have pieces to pick up,
something to hold in your hands, like ticket stubs or change.

But happiness floats.
It doesn't need you to hold it down.
It doesn't need anything.
Happiness lands on the roof of the next house, singing,
and disappears when it wants to.
You are happy either way.
Even the fact that you once lived in a peaceful tree house
and now live over a quarry of noise and dust
cannot make you unhappy.
Everything has a life of its own,
it too could wake up filled with possibilities
of coffee cake and ripe peaches,
and love even the floor which needs to be swept,
the soiled linens and scratched records ...

Since there is no place large enough
to contain so much happiness,
you shrug, you raise your hands, and it flows out of you
into everything you touch. You are not responsible.
You take no credit, as the night sky takes no credit
for the moon, but continues to hold it, and share it,
and in that way, be known.

18 may

To the Evening Star
William Blake (1757–1827)

Thou fair-hair'd angel of the evening,
Now, whilst the sun rests on the mountains, light
Thy bright torch of love; thy radiant crown
Put on, and smile upon our evening bed!
Smile on our loves, and while thou drawest the
Blue curtains of the sky, scatter thy silver dew
On every flower that shuts its sweet eyes
In timely sleep. Let thy west wind sleep on
The lake; speak silence with thy glimmering eyes,
And wash the dusk with silver. Soon, full soon,
Dost thou withdraw; then the wolf rages wide,
And the lion glares thro' the dun forest:
The fleeces of our flocks are cover'd with
Thy sacred dew: protect them with thine influence.

19 may

The Growth of Love XI
Archibald Lampman (1861-1899)

Belovèd, those who moan of love's brief day
Shall find but little grace with me, I guess,
Who know too well this passion's tenderness
To deem that it shall lightly pass away,
A moment's interlude in life's dull play;
Though many loves have lingered to distress,
So shall not ours, sweet Lady, ne'ertheless,
But deepen with us till both heads be grey.
For perfect love is like a fair green plant,
That fades not with its blossoms, but lives on,
And gentle lovers shall not come to want,
Though fancy with its first mad dream be gone;
Sweet is the flower, whose radiant glory flies,
But sweeter still the green that never dies.

20 may

'Move eastward, happy earth'
Alfred, Lord Tennyson (1809–1892)

Move eastward, happy earth, and leave
    Yon orange sunset waning slow:
From fringes of the faded eve,
    O, happy planet, eastward go;
Till over thy dark shoulder glow
    Thy silver sister-world, and rise
    To glass herself in dewy eyes
That watch me from the glen below.

Ah, bear me with thee, smoothly borne,
    Dip forward under starry light,
And move me to my marriage-morn,
    And round again to happy night.

21 may

A Nocturnal Reverie (extract)
Anne Finch, Countess of Winchilsea (1661–1720)

When nibbling sheep at large pursue their food,
And unmolested kine rechew the cud;
When curlews cry beneath the village walls,
And to her straggling brood the partridge calls;
Their shortlived jubilee the creatures keep,
Which but endures, whilst tyrant man does sleep;
When a sedate content the spirit feels,
And no fierce light disturbs, whilst it reveals;
But silent musings urge the mind to seek
Something, too high for syllables to speak;
Till the free soul to a composedness charmed,
Finding the elements of rage disarmed,
O'er all below a solemn quiet grown,
Joys in th' inferior world, and thinks it like her own:
In such a night let me abroad remain,
Till morning breaks, and all's confused again;
Our cares, our toils, our clamors are renewed,
Or pleasures, seldom reached, again pursued.

22 may

'Little birds of the night'
Stephen Crane (1871–1900)

Little birds of the night
Aye, they have much to tell
Perching there in rows
Blinking at me with their serious eyes
Recounting of flowers they have seen and loved
Of meadows and groves of the distance
And pale sands at the foot of the sea
And breezes that fly in the leaves.
They are vast in experience
These little birds that come in the night.

23 may

When You Go
Edwin Morgan (1920–2010)

When you go,
if you go,
and I should want to die,
there's nothing I'd be saved by
more than the time
you fell asleep in my arms
in a trust so gentle
I let the darkening room
drink up the evening, till
rest, or the new rain
lightly roused you awake.
I asked if you heard the rain in your dream
and half dreaming still you only said, I love you.

24 may

Dream Pedlary (extract)
Thomas Lovell Beddoes (1803-1849)

If there were dreams to sell,
   What would you buy?
Some cost a passing bell;
   Some a light sigh,
That shakes from Life's fresh crown
Only a rose-leaf down.
If there were dreams to sell,
Merry and sad to tell,
And the crier rang the bell,
   What would you buy?

25 may

An Hymn to the Evening
Phillis Wheatley (1753–1784)

Soon as the sun forsook the eastern main,
The pealing thunder shook the heav'nly plain:
Majestic grandeur! From the zephyr's wing
Exhales the incense of the blooming spring.
Soft purl the streams; the birds renew their notes,
And through the air their mingled music floats.
Through all the heav'ns what beauteous dies are spread!
But the west glories in the deepest red:
So may our breasts with ev'ry virtue glow,
The living temples of our God below.
Fill'd with the praise of him who gives the light
And draws the sable curtains of the night,
Let placid slumbers sooth each weary mind
At morn to wake more heav'nly, more refin'd;
So shall the labours of the day begin
More pure, more guarded from the snares of sin.
Night's leaden sceptre seals my drowsy eyes;
Then cease, my song, till fair Aurora rise.

26 may

Peace
Sara Teasdale (1884-1933)

Peace flows into me
   As the tide to the pool by the shore;
   It is mine forevermore,
It ebbs not back like the sea.
I am the pool of blue
   That worships the vivid sky;
   My hopes were heaven-high,
They are all fulfilled in you.
I am the pool of gold
   When sunset burns and dies –
   You are my deepening skies,
Give me your stars to hold.

27 may

Harbor Dawn
Lucy Maud Montgomery (1874-1942)

There's a hush and stillness calm and deep,
For the waves have wooed all the winds to sleep
In the shadow of headlands bold and steep;
But some gracious spirit has taken the cup
Of the crystal sky and filled it up
With rosy wine, and in it afar
Has dissolved the pearl of the morning star.

The girdling hills with the night-mist cold
In purple raiment are hooded and stoled
And smit on the brows with fire and gold;
And in the distance the wide, white sea
Is a thing of glamour and wizardry,
With its wild heart lulled to a passing rest,
And the sunrise cradled upon its breast.

With the first red sunlight on mast and spar
A ship is sailing beyond the bar,
Bound to a land that is fair and far;
And those who wait and those who go
Are brave and hopeful, for well they know
Fortune and favour the ship shall win
That crosses the bar when the dawn comes in.

28 may

'There is no frigate like a book'
Emily Dickinson (1830–1886)

There is no Frigate like a Book
To take us Lands away,
Nor any Coursers like a Page
Of prancing Poetry –
This Travel may the poorest take
Without offense of Toll –
How frugal is the Chariot
That bears the Human soul.

29 may

The Treasure
Rupert Brooke (1887–1915)

When colour goes home into the eyes,
   And lights that shine are shut again,
With dancing girls and sweet bird's cries
   Behind the gateways of the brain;
And that no-place which gave them birth, shall close
The rainbow and the rose: –

Still may Time hold some golden space
   Where I'll unpack that scented store
Of song and flower and sky and face,
   And count, and touch, and turn them o'er,
Musing upon them: as a mother, who
Has watched her children all the rich day through,
Sits, quiet-handed, in the fading light,
When children sleep, ere night.

30 may

Change
Mary Elizabeth Coleridge (1861–1907)

Ah, there is no abiding!
   Signs from heaven are sent.
Over the grass the wind went gliding,
   And the green grass grew silver as he went.

Ah, there is no remaining!
   Ever the tide of ocean ebbs and flows.
Over the blue sea goes the wind complaining,
   And the blue sea turns emerald as he goes.

31 may

Being but Men
Dylan Thomas (1914-1953)

Being but men, we walked into the trees
Afraid, letting our syllables be soft
For fear of waking the rooks,
For fear of coming
Noiselessly into a world of wings and cries.

If we were children we might climb,
Catch the rooks sleeping, and break no twig,
And, after the soft ascent,
Thrust out our heads above the branches
To wonder at the unfailing stars.

Out of confusion, as the way is,
And the wonder, that man knows,
Out of the chaos would come bliss.

That, then, is loveliness, we said,
Children in wonder watching the stars,
Is the aim and the end.

Being but men, we walked into the trees.

june

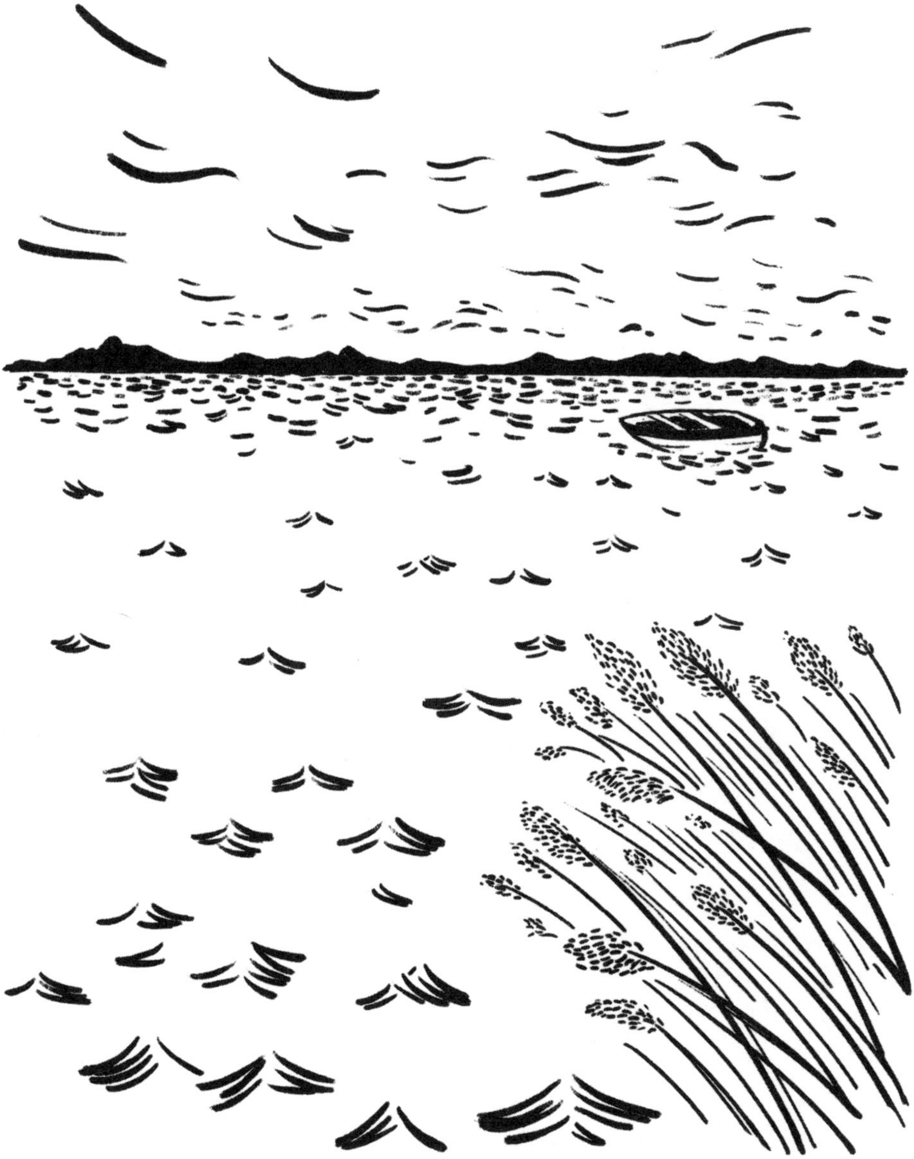

1 june

Rest and Be Thankful! – At the head of Glencroe
William Wordsworth (1770–1850)

Doubling and doubling with laborious walk,
Who, that has gained at length the wished-for Height,
This brief, this simple wayside Call can slight,
And rests not thankful? Whether cheered by talk
With some loved friend, or by the unseen hawk
Whistling to clouds and sky-born streams, that shine
At the sun's outbreak, as with light divine,
Ere they descend to nourish root and stalk
Of valley flowers. Nor, while the limbs repose,
Will we forget that, as the fowl can keep
Absolute stillness, poised aloft in air,
And fishes front, unmoved, the torrent's sweep, –
So may the Soul, through powers that Faith bestows,
Win rest, and ease, and peace, with bliss that Angels share.

2 june

Villa Pauline (extract)
Katherine Mansfield (1888–1923)

But Ah! before he came
You were only a name
Four little rooms and cupboard
Without a bone,
And I was alone!
Now with your windows wide
Everything from outside
Of sun and flower and loveliness
Comes in to hide –
To play, to laugh on the stairs
To catch unawares
Our childish happiness
And to glide
Through the four little rooms on tip toe
With lifted finger,
Pretending we shall not know
When the shutters are shut
That they still linger
Long, long after
Lying close in the dark
He says to me hark,
Isn't that laughter?

3 june

Epithalamion (extract)
Edmund Spenser (c. 1552–1599)

But let stil Silence trew night watches keepe,
That sacred peace may in assurance rayne,
And tymely sleep, when it is tyme to sleepe,
May poure his limbs forth on your pleasant playne,
The whiles an hundred little wingèd loves,
Like divers fethered doves,
Shall fly and flutter round about your bed,
And in the secret darke, that none reproves,
Their prety stealthes shal worke, and snares shal spread
To filch away sweet snatches of delight,
Conceald through covert night.

4 june

Everything Is Going to Be All Right
Derek Mahon (1941–2020)

How should I not be glad to contemplate
the clouds clearing beyond the dormer window
and a high tide reflected on the ceiling?
There will be dying, there will be dying,
but there is no need to go into that.
The lines flow from the hand unbidden
and the hidden source is the watchful heart;
the sun rises in spite of everything
and the far cities are beautiful and bright.
I lie here in a riot of sunlight
watching the day break and the clouds flying.
Everything is going to be all right.

5 june

Yet a Little Sleep
Robert Fuller Murray (1863–1894)

Beside the drowsy streams that creep
Within this island of repose,
Oh, let us rest from cares and woes,
Oh, let us fold our hands to sleep!

Is it ignoble, then, to keep
Awhile from where the rough wind blows,
And all is strife, and no man knows
What end awaits him on the deep?

The voyager may rest awhile,
When rest invites, and yet may be
Neither a sluggard nor a craven.
With strength renewed he quits the isle,
And putting out again to sea,
Makes sail for his desired haven.

6 june

A Sleeping Priestess of Aphrodite (extract)
Robert Cameron Rogers (1862–1912)

She dreams of Love upon the temple stair, –
   About her feet the lithe green lizards play
In all the drowsy, warm, Sicilian air.

The winds have loosed the fillet from her hair,
   Sea winds, salt-lipped, that laugh and seem to say,
'She dreams of Love, upon the temple stair.

'Then let us twine soft fingers, here and there,
   Amid the gleaming threads that drift and stray
In all the drowsy, warm Sicilian air,

'And let us weave of them a subtle snare
   To cast about and bind her, as to-day
She dreams of Love, upon the temple stair.'

They bound her sleeping, in her own bright hair,
   And as she slept came Love – and passed away, –
She dreams of Love, upon the temple stair.

7 june

'The sun has long been set'
William Wordsworth (1770–1850)

The sun has long been set,
   The stars are out by twos and threes,
The little birds are piping yet
   Among the bushes and trees;
There's a cuckoo, and one or two thrushes,
And a far-off wind that rushes,
And a sound of water that gushes,
And the cuckoo's sovereign cry
Fills all the hollow of the sky.
   Who would go 'parading'
In London, and 'masquerading',
On such a night of June
With that beautiful soft half-moon,
And all these innocent blisses?
On such a night as this is!

8 june

Lochan
Kathleen Jamie (b. 1962)
(for Jean Johnstone)

When all this is over I mean
to travel north, by the high

drove roads and cart tracks
probably in June,

with the gentle dog-roses
flourishing beside me. I mean

to find among the thousands
scattered in that land

a certain lochan,
where water lilies rise

like small fat moons,
and tied among the reeds,

underneath a rowan,
a white boat waits.

9 june

There Is a Field (extract)
Rumi (1207–1273)

Out beyond ideas of wrongdoing
And rightdoing there is a field.
I'll meet you there.
When the soul lies down in that grass
The world is too full to talk about.

10 june

Bed in Summer
Robert Louis Stevenson (1850–1894)

In winter I get up at night
And dress by yellow candle-light.
In summer, quite the other way,
I have to go to bed by day.

I have to go to bed and see
The birds still hopping on the tree,
Or hear the grown-up people's feet
Still going past me in the street.

And does it not seem hard to you,
When all the sky is clear and blue,
And I should like so much to play,
To have to go to bed by day?

11 june

Ode to Psyche (extract)
John Keats (1795–1821)

O brightest! though too late for antique vows,
   Too, too late for the fond believing lyre,
When holy were the haunted forest boughs,
   Holy the air, the water, and the fire;
Yet even in these days so far retired
   From happy pieties, thy lucent fans,
   Fluttering among the faint Olympians,
I see, and sing, by my own eyes inspired.
So let me be thy choir, and make a moan
   Upon the midnight hours;
Thy voice, thy lute, thy pipe, thy incense sweet
   From swingèd censer teeming;
Thy shrine, thy grove, thy oracle, thy heat
   Of pale-mouthed prophet dreaming.

Yes, I will be thy priest, and build a fane
    In some untrodden region of my mind,
Where branched thoughts, new grown with pleasant pain,
    Instead of pines shall murmur in the wind:
Far, far around shall those dark-clustered trees
    Fledge the wild-ridgèd mountains steep by steep;
And there by zephyrs, streams, and birds, and bees,
    The moss-lain Dryads shall be lulled to sleep;
And in the midst of this wide quietness
A rosy sanctuary will I dress
With the wreathed trellis of a working brain,
    With buds, and bells, and stars without a name,
With all the gardener Fancy e'er could feign,
    Who breeding flowers, will never breed the same:
And there shall be for thee all soft delight
    That shadowy thought can win,
A bright torch, and a casement ope at night,
    To let the warm Love in!

12 june

The Lotos-Eaters (extract)
Alfred, Lord Tennyson (1809-1892)

There is sweet music here that softer falls
Than petals from blown roses on the grass,
Or night-dews on still waters between walls
Of shadowy granite, in a gleaming pass;
Music that gentlier on the spirit lies,
Than tir'd eyelids upon tir'd eyes;
Music that brings sweet sleep down from the blissful skies.
Here are cool mosses deep,
And thro' the moss the ivies creep,
And in the stream the long-leaved flowers weep
And from the craggy ledge the poppy hangs in sleep.

13 june

A Midsummer Night's Dream Act 5, Scene 1 (extract)
William Shakespeare (c. 1564–1616)

The iron tongue of midnight hath told twelve.
Lovers, to bed; 'tis almost fairy time.
I fear we shall outsleep the coming morn
As much as we this night have overwatched.
This palpable-gross play hath well beguiled
The heavy gait of night. Sweet friends, to bed.

14 june

Faithful Pollinator
Sarah Watkinson

I seem to have lost my interest in the moon.
A scent I've never met, but half-remember
rises from the forest. I meander
aimless at first, until it calls me down

through a dark of sodden bark and umber
fluttering through tangles of lianes
on waves of drunken air, antenna-drawn
to my earthbound star. I home-in and surrender:

my tongue unrolls, I feel its lengthly weight
tap a well of nectar, till I'm full
and my floral-other sets me free.

I come to myself, stow tongue and legs, take flight
cast-off from that strange vegetable pull
and rise, moon-charmed again, towards the sky.

15 june

When Lilacs Last in the Dooryard Bloom'd (extract)
Walt Whitman (1819–1892)

From deep secluded recesses,
From the fragrant cedars and the ghostly pines so still,
Came the carol of the bird.

And the charm of the carol rapt me,
As I held as if by their hands my comrades in the night,
And the voice of my spirit tallied the song of the bird.

To the tally of my soul,
Loud and strong kept up the gray-brown bird,
With pure deliberate notes spreading filling the night.
Loud in the pines and cedars dim,
Clear in the freshness moist and swamp-perfume,
And I with my comrades there in the night.

16 june

The Way Through the Woods
Rudyard Kipling (1865-1936)

They shut the road through the woods
Seventy years ago.
Weather and rain have undone it again,
And now you would never know
There was once a road through the woods
Before they planted the trees.
It is underneath the coppice and heath,
And the thin anemones.
Only the keeper sees
That, where the ring-dove broods,
And the badgers roll at ease,
There was once a road through the woods.

Yet, if you enter the woods
Of a summer evening late,
When the night-air cools on the trout-ringed pools
Where the otter whistles his mate,
(They fear not men in the woods,
Because they see so few.)
You will hear the beat of a horse's feet,
And the swish of a skirt in the dew,
Steadily cantering through
The misty solitudes,
As though they perfectly knew
The old lost road through the woods.
But there is no road through the woods.

17 june

Villanelle of Sunset
Ernest Dowson (1867–1900)

Come hither, child, and rest,
This is the end of day,
Behold the weary West!

Sleep rounds with equal zest
Man's toil and children's play,
Come hither, child, and rest.

My white bird, seek thy nest,
Thy drooping head down lay,
Behold the weary West!

Now eve is manifest
And homeward lies our way,
Behold the weary West!

Tired flower! upon my breast
I would wear thee alway,
Come hither, child, and rest –
Behold the weary West!

18 june

'And death shall have no dominion'
Dylan Thomas (1914-1953)

And death shall have no dominion.
Dead men naked they shall be one
With the man in the wind and the west moon;
When their bones are picked clean and the clean bones gone,
They shall have stars at elbow and foot;
Though they go mad they shall be sane,
Though they sink through the sea they shall rise again;
Though lovers be lost love shall not;
And death shall have no dominion.

And death shall have no dominion.
Under the windings of the sea
They lying long shall not die windily;
Twisting on racks when sinews give way,
Strapped to a wheel, yet they shall not break;
Faith in their hands shall snap in two,
And the unicorn evils run them through;
Split all ends up they shan't crack;
And death shall have no dominion.

And death shall have no dominion.
No more may gulls cry at their ears
Or waves break loud on the seashores;
Where blew a flower may a flower no more
Lift its head to the blows of the rain;
Though they be mad and dead as nails,
Heads of the characters hammer through daisies;
Break in the sun till the sun breaks down,
And death shall have no dominion.

19 june

Travelling
William Wordsworth (1770–1850)

This is the spot:– how mildly does the sun
Shine in between the fading leaves! the air
In the habitual silence of this wood
Is more than silent: and this bed of heath,
Where shall we find so sweet a resting-place?
Come! – let me see thee sink into a dream
Of quiet thoughts, – protracted till thine eye
Be calm as water when the winds are gone
And no one can tell whither. – my sweet friend!
We two have had such happy hours together
That my heart melts in me to think of it.

20 june

'Soon will the high Midsummer pomps come on'
Matthew Arnold (1822-1888)

Soon will the high Midsummer pomps come on,
   Soon will the musk carnations break and swell,
Soon shall we have gold-dusted snapdragon,
   Sweet-William with his homely cottage-smell,
   And stocks in fragrant blow;
Roses that down the alleys shine afar,
   And open, jasmine-muffled lattices,
   And groups under the dreaming garden-trees,
And the full moon, and the white evening-star.

21 june

The Unknown Bird
Edward Thomas (1878–1917)

Three lovely notes he whistled, too soft to be heard
If others sang; but others never sang
In the great beech-wood all that May and June.
No one saw him: I alone could hear him
Though many listened. Was it but four years
Ago? or five? He never came again.

Oftenest when I heard him I was alone,
Nor could I ever make another hear.
La-la-la! he called, seeming far-off –
As if a cock crowed past the edge of the world,
As if the bird or I were in a dream.
Yet that he travelled through the trees and sometimes
Neared me, was plain, though somehow distant still
He sounded. All the proof is – I told men
What I had heard.

                              I never knew a voice,
Man, beast, or bird, better than this. I told
The naturalists; but neither had they heard
Anything like the notes that did so haunt me,
I had them clear by heart and have them still.
Four years, or five, have made no difference. Then
As now that La-la-la! was bodiless sweet:
Sad more than joyful it was, if I must say
That it was one or other, but if sad
'Twas sad only with joy too, too far off
For me to taste it. But I cannot tell
If truly never anything but fair
The days were when he sang, as now they seem.
This surely I know, that I who listened then,
Happy sometimes, sometimes suffering
A heavy body and a heavy heart,
Now straightway, if I think of it, become
Light as that bird wandering beyond my shore.

22 june

A Midsummer Night's Dream Act 2,
Scene 1 (extract)
William Shakespeare (c. 1564–1616)

I know a bank where the wild thyme blows,
Where oxlips and the nodding violet grows,
Quite over-canopied with luscious woodbine,
With sweet muskroses and with eglantine.
There sleeps Titania sometime of the night,
Lulled in these flowers with dances and delight.
And there the snake throws her enamelled skin,
Weed wide enough to wrap a fairy in.

23 june

Night (extract)
Augusta Cooper Bristol (1835–1910)

I stood and watched the still, mysterious Night,
Steal from her shadowy caverns in the East,
To work her deep enchantments on the world.
Her black veil floated down the silent glens,
While her dark sandalled feet, with noiseless tread,
Moved to a secret harmony. Along
The brows of the majestic hills, she strung
Her glorious diamonds so stealthily,
It never marred their dreams; and in the deep,
Cool thickets of the wood, where scarce the Day
Could reach the dim retreat, her dusky hand
Pinned on the breast of the exhaling flower,
A glittering gem; while all the tangled ferns
And forest lace-work, as she moved along,
Grew moist and shining.
   Who would e'er have guessed,
The queenly Night would deign to stoop and love
A little flower! And yet, with all her stealth,
I saw her press her damp and cooling lip
Upon the feverish bosom of a Rose;
At which a watchful bird poured sudden forth
A love-sick song, of sweet and saddest strain.

[cont.]

Upon the ivied rocks, and rugged crags
On which the ocean billows break, she hung
Her sombre mantle; and the gray old sea
That had been high in tumult all the day,
Became so mesmerized beneath her wiles,
He seemed a mere reflection of herself.
The billows sank into a dimpled sleep;
Only the little tide-waves glided up
To kiss the blackness of the airy robe
That floated o'er them.
   Long I stood and watched
The mystic, spell-like influence of Night;
Till o'er the eastern hills, came up the first
Faint glories of the crown that Phoebus wears.
And soon; the Earth, surprised to see the work
That Night had wrought, began to glow and blush,
Like maidens, conscious of the glance of Love.
While she, – the dark Enchantress, – like to one
Who decorates her bower with all things fair,
Wherewith to please her lover? but yet flees
At his approaching step, – at the first gleam
That lit the zenith from the Day-god's eye,
Fled timid o'er the distant western hills.

24 june

Boats in the Bay
Winifred Holtby (1898-1935)

I will take my trouble and wrap it in a blue handkerchief
And carry it down to the sea.
The sea is as smooth as silk, is as silent as glass;
It does not even whisper
Only the boats, rowed out by the girls in yellow
Ruffle its surface.
It is grey, not blue. It is flecked with boats like midges,
With happy people
Moving soundlessly over the level water.

I will take my trouble and drop it into the water
It is heavy as stone and smooth as a sea-washed pebble.
It will sink under the sea, and the happy people
Will row over it quietly, ruffling the clear water
Little dark boats like midges, skimming silently
Will pass backwards and forwards, the girls singing;
They will never know that they have sailed above sorrow.
Sink heavily and lie still, lie still my trouble.

25 june

A Sketch from Nature
John Tupper (c. 1824–1879)

The air blows pure, for twenty miles,
   Over this vast countrié:
Over hill and wood and vale, it goeth,
   Over steeple, and stack, and tree:
And there's not a bird on the wind but knoweth
   How sweet these meadows be.

The swallows are flying beside the wood,
   And the corbies are hoarsely crying;
And the sun at the end of the earth hath stood,
And, thorough the hedge and over the road,
   On the grassy slope is lying:
And the sheep are taking their supper-food
   While yet the rays are dying.

Sleepy shadows are filling the furrows,
   And giant-long shadows the trees are making;
And velvet soft are the woodland tufts,
And misty-grey the low-down crofts;
But the aspens there have gold-green tops,
   And the gold-green tops are shaking:
The spires are white in the sun's last light; –
And yet a moment ere he drops,
Gazes the sun on the golden slopes.

Two sheep, afar from fold,
    Are on the hill-side straying,
With backs all silver, breasts all gold:
    The merle is something saying,
Something very very sweet: –
    'The day – the day – the day is done:'
There answereth a single bleat –
The air is cold, the sky is dimming,
And clouds are long like fishes swimming.

26 june

'Angel spirits of sleep'
Robert Bridges (1844–1930)

Angel spirits of sleep,
White-robed, with silver hair,
In your meadows fair,
Where the willows weep,
And the sad moonbeam
On the gliding stream
Writes her scattered dream:

Angel spirits of sleep,
Dancing to the weir
In the hollow roar
Of its waters deep;
Know ye how men say
That ye haunt no more
Isle and grassy shore
With your moonlit play;
That ye dance not here,
White-robed spirits of sleep,
All the summer night
Threading dances light?

27 june

'There are no gods'
D. H. Lawrence (1885–1930)

There are no gods, and you can please yourself
have a game of tennis, go out in the car, do some shopping, sit and talk,
  talk, talk
with a cigarette browning your fingers.

There are no gods, and you can please yourself –
go and please yourself –

But leave me alone, leave me alone, to myself!
and then in the room, whose is the presence
that makes the air so still and lovely to me?

Who is it that softly touches the sides of my breast
and touches me over the heart
so that my heart beats soothed, soothed, soothed and at peace?

Who is it that smooths the bed-sheets like the cool
smooth ocean where the fishes rest on edge
in their own dream?

Who is it that clasps and kneads my naked feet, till they unfold,
till all is well, till all is utterly well? the lotus-lilies of the feet!

I tell you, it is no woman, it is no man, for I am alone.
And I fall asleep with the gods, the gods
that are not, or that are
according to the soul's desire,
like a pool into which we plunge, or do not plunge.

28 june

Moonlight, Summer Moonlight
Emily Brontë (1818-1848)

'Tis moonlight, summer moonlight,
All soft and still and fair;
The silent time of midnight
Shines sweetly everywhere,

But most where trees are sending
Their breezy boughs on high,
Or stooping low are lending
A shelter from the sky.

29 june

Gitanjali 24–25
Rabindranath Tagore (1861–1941)

If the day is done, if birds sing no more,
if the wind has flagged tired,
then draw the veil of darkness thick upon me,
even as thou hast wrapt the earth with the coverlet of sleep
and tenderly closed the petals of the drooping lotus at dusk.

From the traveller, whose sack of provisions
is empty before the voyage is ended,
whose garment is torn and dust-laden,
whose strength is exhausted,
remove shame and poverty, and renew his life like a flower
under the cover of thy kindly night.

In the night of weariness
let me give myself up to sleep without struggle,
resting my trust upon thee.

Let me not force my flagging spirit
into a poor preparation for thy worship.

It is thou who drawest the veil of night
upon the tired eyes of the day
to renew its sight in a fresher gladness of awakening.

30 june

The Pleiades
Amy Lowell (1874-1925)

By day you cannot see the sky
For it is up so very high.
You look and look, but it's so blue
That you can never see right through.

But when night comes it is quite plain,
And all the stars are there again.
They seem just like old friends to me,
I've known them all my life you see.

There is the dipper first, and there
Is Cassiopeia in her chair,
Orion's belt, the Milky Way,
And lots I know but cannot say.

One group looks like a swarm of bees,
Papa says they're the Pleiades;
But I think they must be the toy
Of some nice little angel boy.

Perhaps his jackstones which to-day
He has forgot to put away,
And left them lying on the sky
Where he will find them bye and bye.

I wish he'd come and play with me.
We'd have such fun, for it would be
A most unusual thing for boys
To feel that they had stars for toys!

july

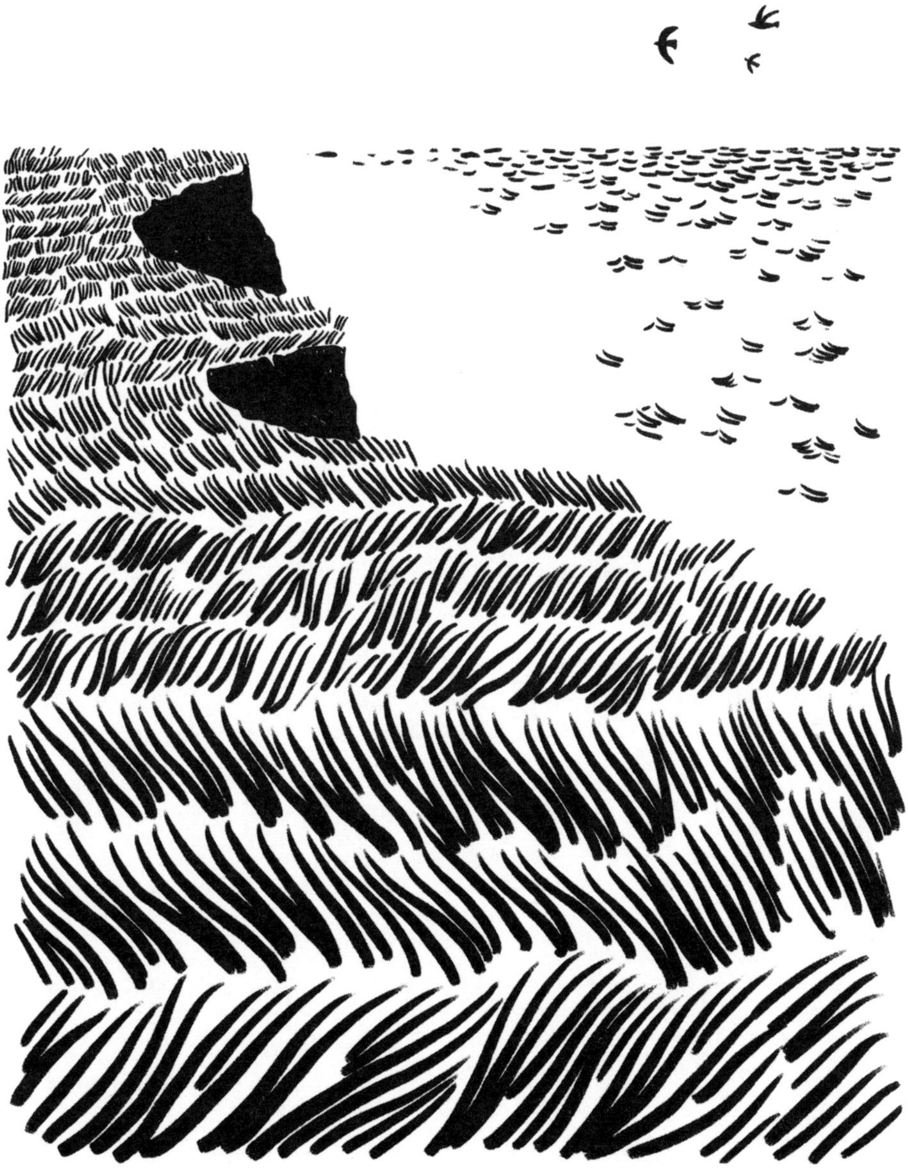

1 july

High Flight
John Gillespie Magee, Jr. (1922-1941)

Oh! I have slipped the surly bonds of Earth
And danced the skies on laughter-silvered wings;
Sunward I've climbed, and joined the tumbling mirth
Of sun-split clouds, and done a hundred things
You have not dreamed of: wheeled and soared and swung
High in the sunlit silence. Hov'ring there,
I've chased the shouting wind along, and flung
My eager craft through footless halls of air . . .
Up, up the long, delirious, burning blue
I've topped the wind-swept heights with easy grace
Where never lark nor even eagle flew
And, while with silent lifting mind I've trod
The high untrespassed sanctity of space,
Put out my hand, and touched the face of God.

2 july

Hymn to the Moon
Written in July, in an Arbour
Lady Mary Wortley Montagu (1689–1762)

Thou silver deity of secret night,
Direct my footsteps through the woodland shade;
Thou conscious witness of unknown delight,
The lover's guardian, and the Muse's aid!

By thy pale beams I solitary rove,
To thee my tender grief confide;
Serenely sweet you gild the silent grove
My friend, my goddess, and my guide.

E'en thee, fair queen, from the amazing height,
The charms of young Endymion drew;
Veiled with the mantle of concealing night,
With all thy greatness, and thy coldness too.

3 july

Vitae Summa Brevis Spem Nos Vetat
Incohare Longam
Ernest Dowson (1867-1900)

They are not long, the weeping and the laughter,
   Love and desire and hate:
I think they have no portion in us after
   We pass the gate.

They are not long, the days of wine and roses:
   Out of a misty dream
Our path emerges for a while, then closes
   Within a dream.

4 july

The New Colossus
Emma Lazarus (1849–1887)

Not like the brazen giant of Greek fame,
With conquering limbs astride from land to land;
Here at our sea-washed, sunset gates shall stand
A mighty woman with a torch, whose flame
Is the imprisoned lightning, and her name
Mother of Exiles. From her beacon-hand
Glows world-wide welcome; her mild eyes command
The air-bridged harbor that twin cities frame.
'Keep, ancient lands, your storied pomp!' cries she
With silent lips. 'Give me your tired, your poor,
Your huddled masses yearning to breathe free,
The wretched refuse of your teeming shore.
Send these, the homeless, tempest-tost to me,
I lift my lamp beside the golden door!'

5 july

Dream Variations
Langston Hughes (1901–1967)

To fling my arms wide
In some place of the sun,
To whirl and to dance
Till the white day is done.
Then rest at cool evening
Beneath a tall tree
While night comes on gently,
   Dark like me –
That is my dream!

To fling my arms wide
In the face of the sun,
Dance! Whirl! Whirl!
Till the quick day is done.
Rest at pale evening . . .
A tall, slim tree . . .
Night coming tenderly
   Black like me.

6 july

The Beds of Fleur-de-lys
Charlotte Perkins Gilman (1860–1935)

High-lying, sea-blown stretches of green turf,
   Wind-bitten close, salt-colored by the sea,
Low curve on curve spread far to the cool sky,
And, curving over them as long they lie,
   Beds of wild fleur-de-lys.

Wide-flowing, self-sown, stealing near and far,
   Breaking the green like islands in the sea;
Great stretches at your feet, and spots that bend
Dwindling over the horizon's end, –
   Wild beds of fleur-de-lys.

The light keen wind streams on across the lifts,
   Their wind of western springtime by the sea;
The close turf smiles unmoved, but over her
Is the far-flying rustle and sweet stir
   In beds of fleur-de-lys.

And here and there across the smooth, low grass
   Tall maidens wander, thinking of the sea;
And bend, and bend, with light robes blown aside,
For the blue lily-flowers that bloom so wide, –
   The beds of fleur-de-lys.

7 july

'Warm summer sun'
Mark Twain (1835–1910)

Warm summer sun,
   Shine kindly here,
Warm southern wind,
   Blow softly here.
Green sod above,
   Lie light, lie light.
Good night, dear heart,
   Good night, good night.

8 july

Echoes
Thomas Moore (1779–1852)

How sweet the answer Echo makes
To Music at night
When, roused by lute or horn, she wakes,
And far away o'er lawns and lakes
Goes answering light!

Yet Love hath echoes truer far
And far more sweet
Than e'er, beneath the moonlight's star,
Of horn or lute or soft guitar
The songs repeat.

'Tis when the sigh, – in youth sincere
And only then,
The sigh that's breathed for one to hear –
Is by that one, that only Dear
Breathed back again.

9 july

The Sandman (extract)
Margaret Thomson Janvier (1844-1913)

The rosy clouds float overhead,
The sun is going down;
And now the sandman's gentle tread
Comes stealing through the town.
'White sand, white sand,' he softly cries,
And as he shakes his head,
Straightway there lies on babies' eyes
His gift of shining sand.
Blue eyes, gray eyes, black eyes, and brown,
As shuts the rose, they softly close, when he goes through the town.

From sunny beaches far away –
Yes, in another land –
He gathers up at break of day
His store of shining sand.
No tempests beat that shore remote,
No ships may sail that way;
His little boat alone may float
Within that lovely bay.
Blue eyes, gray eyes, black eyes, and brown,
As shuts the rose, they softly close, when he goes through the town.

So when you hear the sandman's song
Sound through the twilight sweet,
Be sure you do not keep him long
A-waiting in the street.
Lie softly down, dear little head,
Rest quiet, busy hands,
Till by your bed, his good-night said,
He strews the shining sands.
Blue eyes, gray eyes, black eyes, and brown,
As shuts the rose, they softly close, when he goes through the town.

10 july

Seaweed
D. H. Lawrence (1885–1930)

Seaweed sways and sways and swirls
as if swaying were its form of stillness;
and it flushes against fierce rock
it slips over it as shadows do, without hurting itself.

11 july

The Kingfisher
W. H. Davies (1871-1940)

It was the Rainbow gave thee birth,
And left thee all her lovely hues;
And, as her mother's name was Tears,
So runs it in my blood to choose
For haunts the lonely pools, and keep
In company with trees that weep.
Go you and, with such glorious hues,
Live with proud peacocks in green parks;
On lawns as smooth as shining glass,
Let every feather show its marks;
Get thee on boughs and clap thy wings
Before the windows of proud kings.
Nay, lovely Bird, thou art not vain;
Thou hast no proud, ambitious mind;
I also love a quiet place
That's green, away from all mankind;
A lonely pool, and let a tree
Sigh with her bosom over me.

12 july

Hot Sun, Cool Fire
George Peele (1556–1596)

Hot sun, cool fire, tempered with sweet air,
Black shade, fair nurse, shadow my white hair.
Shine, sun; burn, fire; breathe, air, and ease me;
Black shade, fair nurse, shroud me and please me.
Shadow, my sweet nurse, keep me from burning;
Make not my glad cause cause of mourning.
  Let not my beauty's fire
  Inflame unstaid desire,
   Nor pierce any bright eye
   That wandereth lightly.

13 july

Proportion
Amy Lowell (1874–1925)

In the sky there is a moon and stars,
And in my garden there are yellow moths
Fluttering about a white azalea bush.

14 july

The Sea-Shore
Letitia Elizabeth Landon (1802–1838)

I should like to dwell where the deep blue sea
Rock'd to and fro as tranquilly,
As if it were willing the halcyon's nest
Should shelter through summer its beautiful guest.
When a plaining murmur like that of a song,
And a silvery line come the waves along:
Now bathing – now leaving the gentle shore,
Where shining sea-shells lay scattered o'er.

And children wandering along the strand,
With the eager eye and the busy hand,
Heaping the pebbles and green sea-weed,
Like treasures laid up for a time of need.
Or tempting the waves with their daring feet,
To launch, perhaps, some tiny fleet:
Mimicking those which bear afar
The wealth of trade – and the strength of war.

I should love, when the sun-set reddened the foam,
To watch the fisherman's boat come home,
With his well-filled net and glittering spoil:
Well has the noon-tide repaid its toil.
While the ships that lie in the distance away
Catch on their canvas the crimsoning ray,
Like fairy ships in the tales of old,
When the sails they spread were purple and gold.

Then the deep delight of the starry night,
With its shadowy depths and dreamy light:
When far away spreads the boundless sea,
As if it imagined infinity.
Let me hear the winds go singing by,
Lulling the waves with their melody:
While the moon like a mother watches their sleep,
And I ask no home but beside the deep.

15 july

A Memory
Lola Ridge (1873-1941)

I remember
The crackle of the palm trees
Over the mooned white roofs of the town ...
The shining town ...
And the tender fumbling of the surf
On the sulphur-yellow beaches
As we sat ... a little apart ... in the close-pressing night.

The moon hung above us like a golden mango,
And the moist air clung to our faces,
Warm and fragrant as the open mouth of a child
And we watched the out-flung sea
Rolling to the purple edge of the world,
Yet ever back upon itself ...
As we ...

Inadequate night ...
And mooned white memory
Of a tropic sea ...
How softly it comes up
Like an ungathered lily.

16 july

'On the beach at night alone'
Walt Whitman (1819–1892)

On the beach at night alone,
As the old mother sways her to and fro singing her husky song,
As I watch the bright stars shining, I think a thought of the clef of the universes and of the future.
A vast similitude interlocks all,
All spheres, grown, ungrown, small, large, suns, moons, planets,
All distances of place however wide,
All distances of time, all inanimate forms,
All souls, all living bodies though they be ever so different, or in different worlds,
All gaseous, watery, vegetable, mineral processes, the fishes, the brutes,
All nations, colors, barbarisms, civilizations, languages,
All identities that have existed or may exist on this globe, or any globe,
All lives and deaths, all of the past, present, future,
This vast similitude spans them, and always has spann'd,
And shall forever span them and compactly hold and enclose them.

17 july

Sea Slumber-Song
Roden Berkeley Wriothesley Noel (1834-1894)

Sea-birds are asleep,
The world forgets to weep,
Sea murmurs her soft slumber-song
On the shadowy sand
Of this elfin land;
'I, the Mother mild,
Hush thee, O my child,
Forget the voices wild!
Isles in elfin light
Dream, the rocks and caves,
Lull'd by whispering waves,
Veil their marbles bright,
Foam glimmers faintly white
Upon the shelly sand
Of this elfin land;
Sea-sound. like violins,
To slumber woos and wins,
I murmur my soft slumber-song,
Leave woes. and wails, and sins,
Ocean's shadowy might
Breathes good-night,
    Good-night!'

18 july

Ebbtide at Sundown
**'Michael Field': Katharine Bradley (1846–1914)
and Edith Cooper (1862–1913)**

How larger is remembrance than desire!
How deeper than all longing is regret!
The tide is gone, the sands are rippled yet;
The sun is gone; the hills are lifted higher,
Crested with rose. Ah, why should we require
Sight of the sea, the sun? The sands are wet,
And in their glassy flaws huge record set
Of the ebbed stream, the little ball of fire.
Gone, they are gone! But, oh, so freshly gone,
So rich in vanishing we ask not where –
So close upon us is the bliss that shone,
And, oh, so thickly it impregns the air!
Closer in beating heart we could not be
To the sunk sun, the far, surrendered sea.

19 july

Subway Wind
Claude McKay (1889-1948)

Far down, down through the city's great gaunt gut
   The gray train rushing bears the weary wind;
In the packed cars the fans the crowd's breath cut,
   Leaving the sick and heavy air behind.
And pale-cheeked children seek the upper door
   To give their summer jackets to the breeze;
Their laugh is swallowed in the deafening roar
   Of captive wind that moans for fields and seas;
Seas cooling warm where native schooners drift
   Through sleepy waters, while gulls wheel and sweep,
Waiting for windy waves the keels to lift
   Lightly among the islands of the deep;
Islands of lofty palm trees blooming white
   That lend their perfume to the tropic sea,
Where fields lie idle in the dew-drenched night,
   And the Trades float above them fresh and free.

20 july

'A ship, an isle, a sickle moon'
James Elroy Flecker (1884-1915)

A Ship, an isle, a sickle moon –
With few but with how splendid stars
The mirrors of the sea are strewn
Between their silver bars!
An isle beside an isle she lay,
The pale ship anchored in the bay,
While in the young moon's port of gold
A star-ship – as the mirrors told –
Put forth its great and lonely light
to the unreflecting Ocean, Night.
And still, a ship upon her seas,
The isle and the island cypresses
Went sailing on without the gale:
And still there moved the moon so pale,
A crescent ship without a sail!

21 july

A Summer Eve's Vision (extract)
Maria Jane Jewsbury (1800–1833)

I heard last night a lovely lute,
   I heard it in the sunset hour,
When every jarring sound was mute,
   And golden light bathed field and flower.

I saw the hills in bright repose,
   And far away a silent sea,
Whilst nearer hamlet-homes arose,
   Each sheltered by its guardian tree.

O'er all was spread a soft blue sky,
   And where the distant waters rolled,
Type of the blest abodes on high
   Swept the sun's path of pearl and gold.

I turned me from a gentle throng,
   Night stilled the lute and quenched the beam,
But sunset and the voice of song
   Pursued me – and I slept to dream.

22 july

A Summer's Night
Paul Laurence Dunbar (1872-1906)

The night is dewy as a maiden's mouth,
    The skies are bright as are a maiden's eyes,
    Soft as a maiden's breath, the wind that flies
Up from the perfumed bosom of the South.
Like sentinels, the pines stand in the park;
    And hither hastening like rakes that roam,
    With lamps to light their wayward footsteps home,
The fire-flies come stagg'ring down the dark.

23 july

The Hill Summit
Dante Gabriel Rossetti (1828–1882)

This feast-day of the sun, his altar there
   In the broad west has blazed for vesper-song;
   And I have loitered in the vale too long
And gaze now a belated worshipper.
Yet may I not forget that I was 'ware,
   So journeying, of his face at intervals
   Transfigured where the fringed horizon falls,
A fiery bush with coruscating hair.

And now that I have climbed and won this height,
   I must tread downward through the sloping shade
And travel the bewildered tracks till night.
   Yet for this hour I still may here be stayed
   And see the gold air and the silver fade
And the last bird fly into the last light.

24 july

One Night
Lizette Woodworth Reese (1856–1935)

One lily scented all the dark. It grew
Down the drenched walk a spike of ghostly white.
Fine, sweet, sad noises thrilled the tender night,
From insects couched on blades that dripped with dew.
The road beyond, cleaving the great fields through,
Echoed no footstep; like a streak of light,
The gaunt and blossoming elder gleamed in sight.
The boughs began to quake, and warm winds blew,
And whirled a myriad petals down the air.
An instant, peaked and black the old house stood;
The next, its gables showed a tremulous gray,
Then deepening gold; the next, the world lay bare!
The moon slipped out the leash of the tall wood,
And through the heavenly meadows fled away.

25 july

Casa Guidi Windows (extract)
Elizabeth Barrett Browning (1806–1861)

I heard last night a little child go singing
   'Neath Casa Guidi windows, by the church,
O bella libertà, O bella! Stringing
   The same words still on notes he went in search
So high for, you concluded the upspringing
   Of such a nimble bird to sky from perch
Must leave the whole bush in a tremble green,
   And that the heart of Italy must beat,
While such a voice had leave to rise serene
   'Twixt church and palace of a Florence street!
A little child, too, who not long had been
   By mother's finger steadied on his feet,
And still *O bella libertà* he sang.

26 july

Moonrise
Gerard Manley Hopkins (1844–1889)

I awoke in the Midsummer not to call night, in the white and the walk
   of the morning:
The moon, dwindled and thinned to the fringe of a fingernail held to
   the candle,
Or paring of paradisïacal fruit, lovely in waning but lustreless,
Stepped from the stool, drew back from the barrow, of dark Maenefa
   the mountain;
A cusp still clasped him, a fluke yet fanged him, entangled him, not
   quit utterly.
This was the prized, the desirable sight, unsought, presented so easily,
Parted me leaf and leaf, divided me, eyelid and eyelid of slumber.

27 july

Dzoka (Return)
Belinda Zhawi (b. 1992)

In the day,
hike this mountain
to find that place
to call home

where you can lay
your tired bones
& spread them
under the sun.

When it sets –
swallow up these nights.
With their clusters of stars,

swallow up these nights
that remind you of home
and its nights
around fires

   and the moon
as a woman,
with the small child on her back,
   singing …

Dzoka haungafe
   Dzoka haungatye
   Kufa haungafe
Kutya haungatye
   Dzoka
   Kufa kutya
Dzoka, dzoka-a, dzoka
haungafe,
   dzoka haungatye.
Kufa kutya – dozoka-a

In the day, hike this mountain
to find that place to call home
where you can lay your tired bones
& spread them under
   the sun

28 july

The Aeolian Harp (extract)
Composed at Clevedon, Somersetshire
Samuel Taylor Coleridge (1772-1834)

My pensive Sara! thy soft cheek reclined
Thus on mine arm, most soothing sweet it is
To sit beside our Cot, our Cot o'ergrown
With white-flowered Jasmin, and the broad-leaved Myrtle,
(Meet emblems they of Innocence and Love!)
And watch the clouds, that late were rich with light,
Slow saddening round, and mark the star of eve
Serenely brilliant (such should Wisdom be)
Shine opposite! How exquisite the scents
Snatched from yon bean-field! and the world so hushed!
The stilly murmur of the distant Sea
Tells us of silence.

                And that simplest Lute,
Placed length-ways in the clasping casement, hark!
How by the desultory breeze caressed,
Like some coy maid half yielding to her lover,
It pours such sweet upbraiding, as must needs
Tempt to repeat the wrong! And now, its strings
Boldlier swept, the long sequacious notes
Over delicious surges sink and rise,
Such a soft floating witchery of sound
As twilight Elfins make, when they at eve
Voyage on gentle gales from Fairy-Land,
Where Melodies round honey-dropping flowers,
Footless and wild, like birds of Paradise,
Nor pause, nor perch, hovering on untamed wing!

O! the one Life within us and abroad,
Which meets all motion and becomes its soul,
A light in sound, a sound-like power in light,
Rhythm in all thought, and joyance everywhere –
Methinks, it should have been impossible
Not to love all things in a world so filled;
Where the breeze warbles, and the mute still air
Is Music slumbering on her instrument.

29 july

The Soldier
Rupert Brooke (1887–1915)

If I should die, think only this of me:
   That there's some corner of a foreign field
That is for ever England. There shall be
   In that rich earth a richer dust concealed;
A dust whom England bore, shaped, made aware,
   Gave, once, her flowers to love, her ways to roam;
A body of England's, breathing English air,
   Washed by the rivers, blest by suns of home.

And think, this heart, all evil shed away,
   A pulse in the eternal mind, no less
     Gives somewhere back the thoughts by England given;
Her sights and sounds; dreams happy as her day;
   And laughter, learnt of friends; and gentleness,
     In hearts at peace, under an English heaven.

30 july

Meeting at Night
Robert Browning (1812-1889)

The grey sea and the long black land;
And the yellow half-moon large and low;
And the startled little waves that leap
In fiery ringlets from their sleep,
As I gain the cove with pushing prow,
And quench its speed i' the slushy sand.

Then a mile of warm sea-scented beach;
Three fields to cross till a farm appears;
A tap at the pane, the quick sharp scratch
And blue spurt of a lighted match,
And a voice less loud, thro' its joys and fears,
Than the two hearts beating each to each!

31 july

'Now sleeps the crimson petal'
Alfred, Lord Tennyson (1809–1892)

   Now sleeps the crimson petal, now the white;
Nor waves the cypress in the palace walk;
Nor winks the gold fin in the porphyry font:
The firefly wakens: waken thou with me.

   Now droops the milkwhite peacock like a ghost,
And like a ghost she glimmers on to me.

   Now lies the Earth all Danaë to the stars,
And all thy heart lies open unto me.

   Now slides the silent meteor on, and leaves
A shining furrow, as thy thoughts in me.

   Now folds the lily all her sweetness up,
And slips into the bosom of the lake:
So fold thyself, my dearest, thou, and slip
Into my bosom and be lost in me.

august

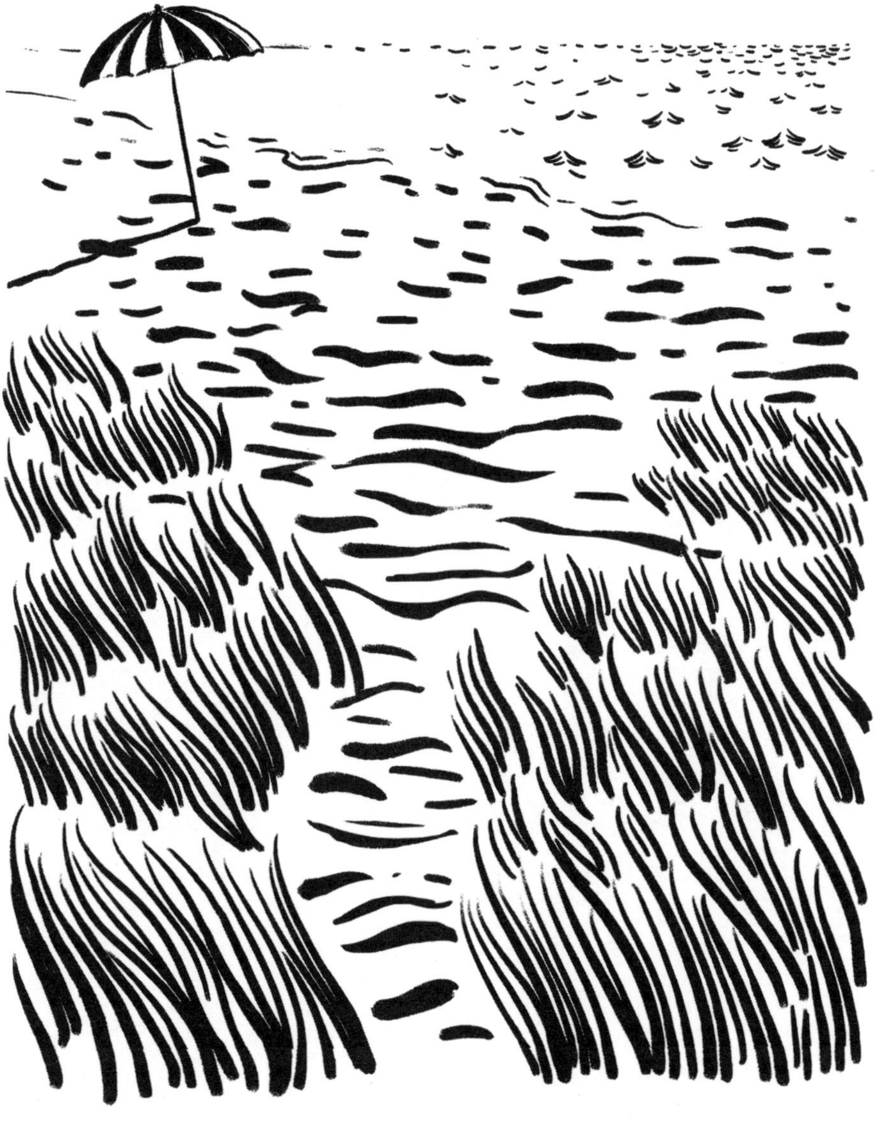

1 august

Fragment of a Sleep-Song
Sydney Dobell (1824–1874)

Sister Simplicitie,
Sing, sing a song to me,
Sing me to sleep.
Some legend low and long
Slow as the summer song
Of the dull Deep.

Some legend long and low,
Whose equal ebb and flow
To and fro creep
On the dim marge of gray
'Tween the soul's night and day,
Washing 'awake' away
Into 'asleep'.

Some legend low and long,
Never so weak or strong
As to let go
While it can hold this heart
Withouten sigh or smart,
Or as to hold this heart
When it sighs 'No'.

Some long low swaying song,
As the sway'd shadow long
Sways to and fro
Where, thro' the crowing cocks,
And by the swinging clocks,
Some weary mother rocks
Some weary woe.

Sing up and down to me
Like a dream-boat at sea,
So, and still so,
Float through the 'then' and 'when',
Rising from when to then,
Sinking from then to when
While the waves go.

Low and high, high and low,
Now and then, then and now,
Mow, now;
And when the now is then, and when the then is now,
And when the low is high, and when the high is low,
Low, low;
Let me float, let the boat
Go, go;
Let me glide, let me slide
Slow, slow;
Gliding boat, sliding boat,
Slow, slow;
Glide away, slide away
So, so.

2 august

The Peace of Wild Things
Wendell Berry (b. 1934)

When despair for the world grows in me
and I wake in the night at the least sound
in fear of what my life and my children's lives may be,
I go and lie down where the wood drake
rests in his beauty on the water, and the great heron feeds.
I come into the peace of wild things
who do not tax their lives with forethought
of grief. I come into the presence of still water.
And I feel above me the day-blind stars
waiting with their light. For a time
I rest in the grace of the world, and am free.

3 august

Titus Andronicus Act 2, Scene 3 (extract)
William Shakespeare (c. 1564–1616)

My lovely Aaron, wherefore look'st thou sad,
When everything doth make a gleeful boast?
The birds chant melody on every bush,
The snake lies rollèd in the cheerful sun,
The green leaves quiver with the cooling wind
And make a chequered shadow on the ground.
Under their sweet shade, Aaron, let us sit,
And whilst the babbling echo mocks the hounds,
Replying shrilly to the well-tuned horns,
As if a double hunt were heard at once,
Let us sit down and mark their yelping noise.
And after conflict such as was supposed
The wand'ring prince and Dido once enjoyed,
When with a happy storm they were surprised
And curtained with a counsel-keeping cave,
We may, each wreathèd in the other's arms,
Our pastimes done, possess a golden slumber,
Whiles hounds and horns and sweet melodious birds
Be unto us as is a nurse's song
Of lullaby to bring her babe asleep.

4 *august*

Fern Hill
Dylan Thomas (1914-1953)

Now as I was young and easy under the apple boughs
About the lilting house and happy as the grass was green,
   The night above the dingle starry,
      Time let me hail and climb
   Golden in the heydays of his eyes,
And honoured among wagons I was prince of the apple towns
And once below a time I lordly had the trees and leaves
      Trail with daisies and barley
   Down the rivers of the windfall light.

And as I was green and carefree, famous among the barns
About the happy yard and singing as the farm was home,
   In the sun that is young once only,
      Time let me play and be
   Golden in the mercy of his means,
And green and golden I was huntsman and herdsman, the calves
Sang to my horn, the foxes on the hills barked clear and cold,
      And the sabbath rang slowly
   In the pebbles of the holy streams.

All the sun long it was running, it was lovely, the hay
Fields high as the house, the tunes from the chimneys, it was air
   And playing, lovely and watery
      And fire green as grass.
   And nightly under the simple stars
As I rode to sleep the owls were bearing the farm away,
All the moon long I heard, blessed among stables, the night-jars
      Flying with the ricks, and the horses
         Flashing into the dark.

And then to awake, and the farm, like a wanderer white
With the dew, come back, the cock on his shoulder: it was all
   Shining, it was Adam and maiden,
     The sky gathered again
   And the sun grew round that very day.
So it must have been after the birth of the simple light
In the first, spinning place, the spellbound horses walking warm
   Out of the whinnying green stable
     On to the fields of praise.

And honoured among foxes and pheasants by the gay house
Under the new made clouds and happy as the heart was long,
   In the sun born over and over,
     I ran my heedless ways,
   My wishes raced through the house high hay
And nothing I cared, at my sky blue trades, that time allows
In all his tuneful turning so few and such morning songs
   Before the children green and golden
     Follow him out of grace,

Nothing I cared, in the lamb white days, that time would take me
Up to the swallow thronged loft by the shadow of my hand,
   In the moon that is always rising,
     Nor that riding to sleep
   I should hear him fly with the high fields
And wake to the farm forever fled from the childless land.
Oh as I was young and easy in the mercy of his means,
   Time held me green and dying
     Though I sang in my chains like the sea.

5 *augus*t

Paper Boats
Rabindranath Tagore (1861-1941)

Day by day I float my paper boats one by one down the running stream.
In big black letters I write my name on them and the name of the village where I live.
I hope that someone in some strange land will find them and know who I am.
I load my little boats with shiuli flowers from our garden, and hope that these blooms of the dawn will be carried safely to land in the night.
I launch my paper boats and look into the sky and see the little clouds setting their white bulging sails.
I know not what playmate of mine in the sky sends them down the air to race with my boats!
When night comes I bury my face in my arms and dream that my paper boats float on and on under the midnight stars.
The fairies of sleep are sailing in them, and the lading is their baskets full of dreams.

6 august

The Recollection (extract)
Percy Bysshe Shelley (1792-1822)

We wander'd to the Pine Forest
   That skirts the Ocean's foam;
The lightest wind was in its nest,
   The tempest in its home.
The whispering waves were half asleep,
   The clouds were gone to play,
And on the bosom of the deep
   The smile of Heaven lay;
It seem'd as if the hour were one
   Sent from beyond the skies
Which scatter'd from above the sun
   A light of Paradise!

We paused amid the pines that stood
   The giants of the waste,
Tortured by storms to shapes as rude
   As serpents interlaced, –
And soothed by every azure breath
   That under heaven is blown
To harmonies and hues beneath,
   As tender as its own:
Now all the tree-tops lay asleep
   Like green waves on the sea,
As still as in the silent deep
   The ocean-woods may be.

[cont.]

How calm it was! – the silence there
    By such a chain was bound,
That even the busy woodpecker
    Made stiller by her sound
The inviolable quietness;
    The breath of peace we drew
With its soft motion made not less
    The calm that round us grew.
There seem'd from the remotest seat
    Of the wide mountain waste
To the soft flower beneath our feet
    A magic circle traced,
A spirit interfused around,
    A thrilling silent life;
To momentary peace it bound
    Our mortal nature's strife; –
And still I felt the centre of
    The magic circle there
Was one fair Form that fill'd with love
    The lifeless atmosphere.

7 august

Silent Noon
Dante Gabriel Rossetti (1828–1882)

Your hands lie open in the long fresh grass, –
The finger-points look through like rosy blooms:
Your eyes smile peace. The pasture gleams and glooms
'Neath billowing skies that scatter and amass.
All round our nest, far as the eye can pass,
Are golden kingcup fields with silver edge
Where the cow-parsley skirts the hawthorn-hedge.
'Tis visible silence, still as the hour-glass.

Deep in the sun-searched growths the dragon-fly
Hangs like a blue thread loosened from the sky:–
So this wing'd hour is dropt to us from above.
Oh! clasp we to our hearts, for deathless dower,
This close-companioned inarticulate hour
When two-fold silence was the song of love.

8 august

A Strip of Blue (extract)
Lucy Larcom (1824–1893)

I do not own an inch of land,
  But all I see is mine, –
The orchard and the mowing-fields,
  The lawns and gardens fine.
The winds my tax-collectors are,
  They bring me tithes divine, –
Wild scents and subtle essences,
  A tribute rare and free;
And, more magnificent than all,
  My window keeps for me
A glimpse of blue immensity, –
  A little strip of sea.

Richer am I than he who owns
  Great fleets and argosies;
I have a share in every ship
  Won by the inland breeze,
To loiter on yon airy road
  Above the apple-trees.
I freight them with my untold dreams;
  Each bears my own picked crew;
And nobler cargoes wait for them
  Than ever India knew, –
My ships that sail into the East
  Across that outlet blue.

Sometimes they seem like living shapes, –
   The people of the sky, –
Guests in white raiment coming down
   From heaven, which is close by;
I call them by familiar names,
   As one by one draws nigh.
So white, so light, so spirit-like,
   From violet mists they bloom!
The aching wastes of the unknown
   Are half reclaimed from gloom,
Since on life's hospitable sea
   All souls find sailing-room.

9 *august*

Yasmin (A Ghazel)
James Elroy Flecker (1884-1915)

How splendid in the morning grows the lily: with what grace
   he throws
His supplication to the rose: do roses nod the head, Yasmin?

But when the silver dove descends I find the little flower of friends
Whose very name that sweetly ends I say when I have said, Yasmin.

The morning light is clear and cold: I dare not in that light behold
A whiter light, a deeper gold, a glory too far shed, Yasmin.

But when the deep red light of day is level with the lone highway,
And some to Meccah turn to pray, and I toward thy bed, Yasmin;

Or when the wind beneath the moon is drifting like a soul aswoon,
And harping planets talk love's tune with milky wings
   outspread, Yasmin,

Shower down thy love, O burning bright! For one night or the
   other night,
Will come the Gardener in white, and gathered flowers are
   dead, Yasmin.

10 august

L'Allegro (extract)
John Milton (1608-1674)

Thus done the tales, to bed they creep,
By whispering winds soon lulled asleep.
Towered cities please us then,
And the busy hum of men,
Where throngs of knights and barons bold
In weeds of peace high triumphs hold,
With store of ladies, whose bright eyes
Rain influence, and judge the prize
Of wit or arms, while both contend
To win her grace whom all commend.
There let Hymen oft appear
In saffron robe, with taper clear,
And pomp, and feast, and revelry,
With masque and antique pageantry:
Such sights as youthful poets dream
On summer eves by haunted stream.

11 august

'The house was quiet and the world was calm'
Wallace Stevens (1879-1955)

The house was quiet and the world was calm.
The reader became the book; and summer night

Was like the conscious being of the book.
The house was quiet and the world was calm.

The words were spoken as if there was no book,
Except that the reader leaned above the page,

Wanted to lean, wanted much most to be
The scholar to whom his book is true, to whom

The summer night is like a perfection of thought.
The house was quiet because it had to be.

The quiet was part of the meaning, part of the mind:
The access of perfection to the page.

And the world was calm. The truth in a calm world,
In which there is no other meaning, itself

Is calm, itself is summer and night, itself
Is the reader leaning late and reading there.

12 august

The Garden (extract)
Andrew Marvell (1621–1678)

How vainly men themselves amaze
To win the palm, the oak, or bays,
And their uncessant labours see
Crowned from some single herb or tree,
Whose short and narrow vergèd shade
Does prudently their toils upbraid,
While all flow'rs and all trees do close
To weave the garlands of repose.

Fair Quiet, have I found thee here,
And Innocence, thy sister dear?
Mistaken long, I sought you then
In busy companies of men.
Your sacred plants, if here below,
Only among the plants will grow.
Society is all but rude,
To this delicious solitude.

What wondrous life is this I lead!
Ripe apples drop about my head;
The luscious clusters of the vine
Upon my mouth do crush their wine;
The nectarine, and curious peach,
Into my hands themselves do reach;
Stumbling on melons, as I pass,
Ensnared with flowers, I fall on grass.

13 august

'Time flies'
Found on an English Sundial

Time flies, Suns rise
And shadows fall.
Let time go by.
Love is forever over all.

14 august

A Summer Day (extract)
Joanna Baillie (1762–1851)

The varied noises of the cheerful village
By slow degrees now faintly die away,
And more distinct each feeble sound is heard
That gently steals adown the river's bed,
Or through the wood comes with the ruffling breeze.
The white mist rises from the swampy glens,
And from the dappled skirting of the heavens
Looks out the evening star. –
The lover skulking in the neighbouring copse
(Whose half-seen form shown through the thickened air,
Large and majestic, makes the traveller start,
And spreads the story of the haunted grove),
Curses the owl, whose loud ill-omened scream,
With ceaseless spite, robes from his watchful ear
The well-known footsteps of his darling maid;
And, fretful, chases from his face the night-fly,
Who, buzzing round his head, doth often skim,
With fluttering wing, across his glowing cheek:
For all but him in deep and balmy sleep
Forget the toil of the oppressive day;
Shut is the door of every scattered cot,
And silence dwells within.

15 august

Nightfall in the City of Hyderabad
Sarojini Naidu (1879–1949)

See how the speckled sky burns like a pigeon's throat,
Jewelled with embers of opal and peridote.

See the white river that flashes and scintillates,
Curved like a tusk from the mouth of the city-gates.

Hark, from the minaret, how the muezzin's call
Floats like a battle-flag over the city wall.

From trellised balconies, languid and luminous
Faces gleam, veiled in a splendour voluminous.

Leisurely elephants wind through the winding lanes,
Swinging their silver bells hung from their silver chains.

Round the high Char Minar sounds of gay cavalcades
Blend with the music of cymbals and serenades.

Over the city bridge Night comes majestical,
Borne like a queen to a sumptuous festival.

16 august

O Radiant Dark
Extract of a Song from *The Spanish Gypsy*
George Eliot (1819–1880)

Dark the night, with breath all flowers,
And tender broken voice that fills
With ravishment the listening hours:
Whisperings, wooings,
Liquid ripples, and soft ring-dove cooings
In low-toned rhythm that love's aching stills.
Dark the night,
Yet is she bright,
For in her dark she brings the mystic star,
Trembling yet strong as is the voice of love,
From some unknown afar.
O radiant Dark! O darkly-fostered ray!
Thou hast a joy too deep for shallow Day.

17 august

High Summer
Ebenezer Jones (1820-1860)

I never wholly feel that summer is high,
However green the grass, or loud the birds,
However movelessly eye-winking herds
Stand in field ponds, or under large trees lie,
Till I do climb all cultured pastures by,
That hedged by hedgerows studiously fretted trim,
Smile like a lady's face with lace laced prim,
And on some moor or hill that seeks the sky
Lonely and nakedly, – utterly lie down,
And feel the sunshine throbbing on body and limb,
My drowsy brain in pleasant drunkenness swim,
Each rising thought sink back, and dreamily drown,
Smiles creep o'er my face, and smother my lips, and cloy,
Each muscle sink to itself, and separately enjoy.

18 august

'The twilight turns'
James Joyce (1882–1941)

The twilight turns from amethyst
To deep and deeper blue,
The lamp fills with a pale green glow
The trees of the avenue.

The old piano plays an air,
Sedate and slow and gay;
She bends upon the yellow keys,
Her head inclines this way.

Shy thought and grave wide eyes and hands
That wander as they list –
The twilight turns to darker blue
With lights of amethyst.

19 august

Good-night
Paul Laurence Dunbar (1872–1906)

The lark is silent in his nest,
The breeze is sighing in its flight,
Sleep, Love, and peaceful be thy rest.
Good-night, my love, good-night, good-night.
Sweet dreams attend thee in thy sleep,
To soothe thy rest till morning's light,
And angels round thee vigil keep.
Good-night, my love, good-night, good-night.
Sleep well, my love, on night's dark breast,
And ease thy soul with slumber bright;
Be joy but thine and I am blest.
Good-night, my love, good-night, good-night.

20 august

The Lake Isle of Innisfree
W. B. Yeats (1865–1939)

I will arise and go now, and go to Innisfree,
And a small cabin build there, of clay and wattles made:
Nine bean-rows will I have there, a hive for the honey-bee;
And live alone in the bee-loud glade.

And I shall have some peace there, for peace comes dropping slow,
Dropping from the veils of the morning to where the cricket sings;
There midnight's all a glimmer, and noon a purple glow,
And evening full of the linnet's wings.

I will arise and go now, for always night and day
I hear lake water lapping with low sounds by the shore;
While I stand on the roadway, or on the pavements grey,
I hear it in the deep heart's core.

21 august

Twilight Calm
Christina Rossetti (1830-1894)

Oh, pleasant eventide!
Clouds on the western side
Glow grey and greyer hiding the warm sun:
The bees and birds, their happy labours done,
Seek their close nests and bide.

Screened in the leafy wood
The stock-doves sit and brood:
The very squirrel leaps from bough to bough
But lazily; pauses; and settles now
Where once he stored his food.

One by one the flowers close,
Lily and dewy rose
Shutting their tender petals from the moon:
The grasshoppers are still; but not so soon
Are still the noisy crows.

The dormouse squats and eats
Choice little dainty bits
Beneath the spreading roots of a broad lime;
Nibbling his fill he stops from time to time
And listens where he sits.

From far the lowings come
Of cattle driven home:
From farther still the wind brings fitfully
The vast continual murmur of the sea,
Now loud, now almost dumb.

The gnats whirl in the air,
The evening gnats; and there
The owl opes broad his eyes and wings to sail
For prey; the bat wakes; and the shell-less snail
Comes forth, clammy and bare.

Hark! that's the nightingale,
Telling the selfsame tale
Her song told when the ancient earth was young:
So echoes answered when her song was sung
In the first wooded vale.

We call it love and pain
The passion of her strain;
And yet we little understand or know:
Why should it not be rather joy that so
Throbs in each throbbing vein?

In separate herds the deer
Lie; here the bucks, and here
The does, and by its mother sleeps the fawn:
Through all the hours of night until the dawn
They sleep, forgetting fear.

[cont.]

The hare sleeps where it lies,
With wary half-closed eyes;
The cock has ceased to crow, the hen to cluck:
Only the fox is out, some heedless duck
Or chicken to surprise.

Remote, each single star
Comes out, till there they are
All shining brightly: how the dews fall damp!
While close at hand the glow-worm lights her lamp
Or twinkles from afar.

But evening now is done
As much as if the sun
Day-giving had arisen in the East:
For night has come; and the great calm has ceased,
The quiet sands have run.

22 august

Sleep
Algernon Charles Swinburne (1837–1909)

Sleep, when a soul that her own clouds cover
Wails that sorrow should always keep
Watch, nor see in the gloom above her
   Sleep,

Down, through darkness naked and steep,
Sinks, and the gifts of his grace recover
Soon the soul, though her wound be deep.

God beloved of us, all men's lover,
All most weary that smile or weep
Feel thee afar or anear them hover,
   Sleep.

23 august

My Bed is a Boat
Robert Louis Stevenson (1850-1894)

My bed is like a little boat;
   Nurse helps me in when I embark;
She girds me in my sailor's coat
   And starts me in the dark.

At night I go on board and say
   Good-night to all my friends on shore;
I shut my eyes and sail away
   And see and hear no more.

And sometimes things to bed I take,
   As prudent sailors have to do;
Perhaps a slice of wedding-cake,
   Perhaps a toy or two.

All night across the dark we steer;
   But when the day returns at last,
Safe in my room, beside the pier,
   I find my vessel fast.

24 august

'Nor rural sights alone, but rural sounds'
William Cowper (1731–1800)

Nor rural sights alone, but rural sounds
Exhilarate the spirit, and restore
The tone of languid nature. Mighty winds
That sweep the skirt of some far-spreading wood
Of ancient growth, make music not unlike
The dash of ocean on his winding shore,
And lull the spirit while they fill the mind,
Unnumbered branches waving in the blast,
And all their leaves fast fluttering, all at once
Nor less composure waits upon the roar
Of distant floods, or on the softer voice
Of neighbouring fountain, or of rills that slip
Through the cleft rock, and chiming as they fall
Upon loose pebbles, lose themselves at length
In matted grass, that with a livelier green
Betrays the secret of their silent course.
Nature inanimate employs sweet sounds,
But animated nature sweeter still
To soothe and satisfy the human ear.
Ten thousand warblers cheer the day, and one
The livelong night: nor these alone whose notes
Nice-fingered art must emulate in vain,
But cawing rooks, and kites that swim sublime

[cont.]

In still repeated circles, screaming loud,
The jay, the pie, and even the boding owl
That hails the rising moon, have charms for me.
Sounds inharmonious in themselves and harsh,
Yet heard in scenes where peace for ever reigns
And only there, please highly for their sake.

25 august

Holidays
Henry Wadsworth Longfellow (1807–1882)

The holiest of all holidays are those
Kept by ourselves in silence and apart;
The secret anniversaries of the heart,
When the full river of feeling overflows; –
The happy days unclouded to their close;
The sudden joys that out of darkness start
As flames from ashes; swift desires that dart
Like swallows singing down each wind that blows!
White as the gleam of a receding sail,
White as a cloud that floats and fades in air,
White as the whitest lily on a stream,
These tender memories are; – a fairy tale
Of some enchanted land we know not where,
But lovely as a landscape in a dream.

26 august

Verses Written in the Chiosk of the British Palace at Pera (extract)
Lady Mary Wortley Montagu (1689–1762)

Yet not these prospects, all profusely gay –
The gilded navy that adorns the sea,
The rising city in confusion fair,
Magnificently formed, irregular,
Where woods and palaces at once surprise,
Gardens on gardens, domes on domes arise,
And endless beauties tire the wandering eyes –
So soothes my wishes, or so charms my mind,
As this retreat, secure from humankind.
No knave's successful craft does spleen excite,
No coxcomb's tawdry splendour shocks my sight,
No mob-alarm awakes my female fears,
No unrewarded merit asks my tears,
Nor praise my mind, nor envy hurts my ear,
Even fame itself can hardly reach me here;
Impertinence, with all her tattling train,
Fair-sounding flattery's delicious bane;
Censorious folly, noisy party rage,
The thousand tongues with which she must engage,
Who dare have virtue in a vicious age.

27 august

The Tempest Act 3, Scene 2 (extract)
William Shakespeare (c. 1564–1616)

Be not afeard. The isle is full of noises,
Sounds, and sweet airs that give delight and hurt not.
Sometimes a thousand twangling instruments
Will hum about mine ears, and sometime voices
That, if I then had waked after long sleep,
Will make me sleep again. And then, in dreaming,
The clouds methought would open and show riches
Ready to drop upon me, that when I waked
I cried to dream again.

28 august

At Set of Sun
Ella Wheeler Wilcox (1850–1919)

If we sit down at set of sun,
And count the things that we have done,
   And, counting, find
One self-denying act, one word
That eased the heart of him who heard,
   One glance, most kind,
That fell like sunshine where it went –
Then we may count that day well spent.

Or, on the other hand, if we,
In looking through the day, can see
   A place or spot
Where we an unkind act put down,
Or where we smiled when wont to frown,
   Or crushed some thought
That cumbered the heart-ground where it stood –
Then we may count that day as good.

But if, through all the life-long day,
We've eased no heart by yea or nay;
   If, through it all
We've done no thing that we can trace,
That brought the sunshine to a face –
   No act most small
That helped some soul, and nothing cost –
Then count that day as worse than lost.

29 august

Evening Song
Sidney Lanier (1842–1881)

Look off, dear Love, across the sallow sands,
And mark yon meeting of the sun and sea,
How long they kiss in sight of all the lands.
Ah! longer, longer, we.

Now in the sea's red vintage melts the sun,
As Egypt's pearl dissolved in rosy wine,
And Cleopatra night drinks all. 'Tis done,
Love, lay thine hand in mine.

Come forth, sweet stars, and comfort heaven's heart;
Glimmer, ye waves, round else unlighted sands.
O night! divorce our sun and sky apart
Never our lips, our hands.

30 august

The Tyger (extract)
William Blake (1757–1827)

Tyger Tyger, burning bright,
In the forests of the night:
What immortal hand or eye,
Could frame thy fearful symmetry?

In what distant deeps or skies
Burnt the fire of thine eyes!
On what wings dare he aspire?
What the hand, dare seize the fire?

When the stars threw down their spears
And water'd heaven with their tears:
Did he smile his work to see?
Did he who made the Lamb make thee?

Tyger, Tyger burning bright,
In the forests of the night:
What immortal hand or eye,
Dare frame thy fearful symmetry?

31 august

Sleep and Poetry (extract)
John Keats (1795–1821)

WHAT is more gentle than a wind in summer?
What is more soothing than the pretty hummer
That stays one moment in an open flower,
And buzzes cheerily from bower to bower?
What is more tranquil than a musk-rose blowing
In a green island, far from all men's knowing?
More healthful than the leafiness of dales?
More secret than a nest of nightingales?
More serene than Cordelia's countenance?
More full of visions than a high romance?
What, but thee Sleep? Soft closer of our eyes!
Low murmurer of tender lullabies!
Light hoverer around our happy pillows!
Wreather of poppy buds, and weeping willows!
Silent entangler of a beauty's tresses!
Most happy listener! when the morning blesses
Thee for enlivening all the cheerful eyes
That glance so brightly at the new sun-rise.

september

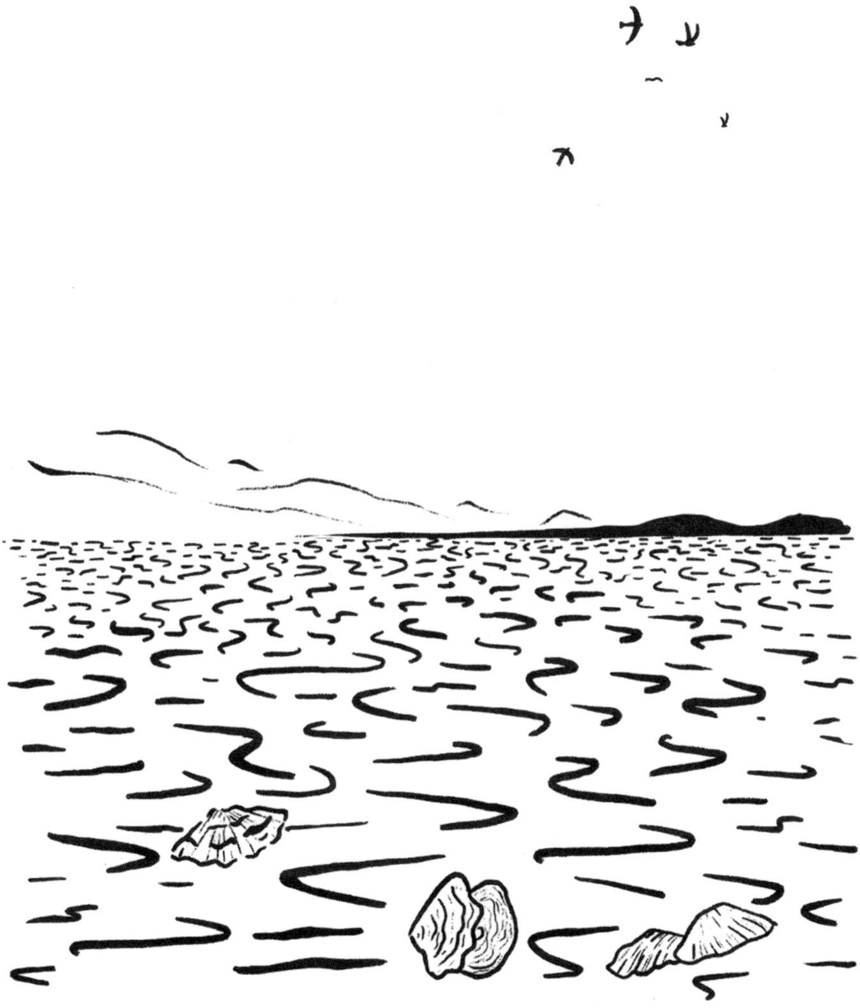

1 september

The Garden of Proserpine (extract)
Algernon Charles Swinburne (1837–1909)

Here, where the world is quiet;
   Here, where all trouble seems
Dead winds' and spent waves' riot
   In doubtful dreams of dreams;
I watch the green field growing
For reaping folk and sowing,
For harvest-time and mowing;
   A sleepy world of streams.

I am tired of tears and laughter,
   And men that laugh and weep;
Of what may come hereafter
   For men that sow to reap;
I am weary of days and hours,
Blown buds of barren flowers,
Desires and dreams and powers
   And everything but sleep.

2 september

Little Boy Blue
Anonymous

Little Boy Blue, come blow your horn,
The sheep's in the meadow, the cow's in the corn;

Where's the little boy that tends the sheep?
He's under the haycock, fast asleep.

Go wake him, go wake him. Oh! no, not I;
For if I awake him, he'll certainly cry.

3 september

Composed Upon Westminster Bridge,
September 3, 1802
William Wordsworth (1770–1850)

Earth has not anything to show more fair:
Dull would he be of soul who could pass by
A sight so touching in its majesty:
This City now doth, like a garment, wear
The beauty of the morning; silent, bare,
Ships, towers, domes, theatres, and temples lie
Open unto the fields, and to the sky;
All bright and glittering in the smokeless air.
Never did sun more beautifully steep
In his first splendour, valley, rock, or hill;
Ne'er saw I, never felt, a calm so deep!
The river glideth at his own sweet will:
Dear God! the very houses seem asleep;
And all that mighty heart is lying still!

4 september

Testimonial
Rita Dove (b. 1952)

Back when the earth was new
and heaven just a whisper,
back when the names of things
hadn't had time to stick;

back when the smallest breezes
melted summer into autumn,
when all the poplars quivered
sweetly in rank and file . . .

the world called, and I answered.
Each glance ignited to a gaze.
I caught my breath and called that life,
swooned between spoonfuls of lemon sorbet.

I was pirouette and flourish,
I was filigree and flame.
How could I count my blessings
when I didn't know their names?

Back when everything was still to come,
luck leaked out everywhere.
I gave my promise to the world,
and the world followed me here.

5 *september*

Sail Away
Rabindranath Tagore (1861-1941)

Early in the day it was whispered that we should sail in a boat,
only thou and I, and never a soul in the world would know of this our
pilgrimage to no country and to no end.

In that shoreless ocean,
at thy silently listening smile my songs would swell in melodies,
free as waves, free from all bondage of words.

Is the time not come yet?
Are there works still to do?
Lo, the evening has come down upon the shore
and in the fading light the seabirds come flying to their nests.

Who knows when the chains will be off,
and the boat, like the last glimmer of sunset,
vanish into the night?

6 september

The Enviable Isles
Herman Melville (1819–1891)

Through storms you reach them and from storms are free.
   Afar descried, the foremost drear in hue,
But, nearer, green; and, on the marge, the sea
   Makes thunder low and mist of rainbowed dew.

But, inland, – where the sleep that folds the hills
A dreamier sleep, the trance Of God, instils, –
   On uplands hazed, in wandering airs aswoon,
Slow-swaying palms salute love's cypress tree
   Adown in vale where pebbly runlets croon
A song to all sorrow and all glee.

Sweet-fern and moss in many a glade are here,
   Where, strown in flocks, what cheek-flushed myriads lie
Dimpling in dream, unconscious slumberers mere,
   While billows endless round the beaches die.

7 september

To the Evening Star
Thomas Campbell (1777-1844)

Star that bringest home the bee,
And sett'st the weary labourer free!
If any shed peace, 'tis Thou
   That send'st it from above,
Appearing when Heaven's breath and brow
   Are sweet as hers we love.

Come to the luxuriant skies,
Whilst the landscape's odours rise,
Whilst far-off lowing herds are heard
   And songs when toil is done,
From cottages whose smoke unstirr'd
   Curls yellow in the sun.

Star of love's soft interviews,
Parted lovers on thee muse;
Their remembrancer in Heaven
   Of thrilling vows thou art,
Too delicious to be riven
   By absence from the heart.

8 september

Wander Song
Anna Wickham (1883-1947)

When I come to the end of the land,
I find the sea,
With edges of cliff and breadths of sand
To pleasure me.

When I raise my town-tired eyes
There is blue and white,
Or kings and castles of stormy skies,
Or joy of night.

When I weary of all I see
And tire even of space,
I hold your love in memory
And your dear face.

9 september

Nightfall
**'Michael Field': Katharine Bradley (1846–1914)
and Edith Cooper (1862–1913)**

She sits beside: through four low panes of glass
The sun, a misty meadow, and the stream;
Falling through rounded elms the last sunbeam.
Through night's thick fibre sudden barges pass
With great forelights of gold, with trailing mass
Of timber: rearward of their transient gleam
The shadows settle, and profounder dream
Enters, fulfils the shadows. Vale and grass
Are now no more; a last leaf strays about,
Then every wandering ceases; we remain.
Clear dusk, the face of wind is on the sky:
The eyes I love to lift to the upper pane –
Their voice gives note of welcome quietly
'I love the air in which the stars come out'.

10 september

'The moon now rises'
Henry David Thoreau (1817–1862)

The moon now rises to her absolute rule,
And the husbandman and hunter
Acknowledge her for their mistress.
Asters and golden reign in the fields
And the life everlasting withers not.
The fields are reaped and shorn of their pride
But an inward verdure still crowns them
The thistle scatters its down on the pool
And yellow leaves clothe the river –
And nought disturbs the serious life of men.
But behind the sheaves and under the sod
There lurks a ripe fruit which the reapers have not gathered
The true harvest of the year – the boreal fruit
Which it bears forever.
With fondness annually watering and maturing it.
But man never severs the stalk
Which bears this palatable fruit.

11 september

'Rocked in the cradle of the deep'
Emma Hart Willard (1787–1870)

Rocked in the cradle of the deep
I lay me down in peace to sleep;
Secure I rest upon the wave,
For thou, O Lord! hast power to save.
I know thou wilt not slight my call,
For Thou dost mark the sparrow's fall;
And calm and peaceful shall I sleep,
Rocked in the cradle of the deep.

When in the dead of night I lie
And gaze upon the trackless sky,
The star-bespangled heavenly scroll,
The boundless waters as they roll, –
I feel thy wondrous power to save
From perils of the stormy wave:
Rocked in the cradle of the deep,
I calmly rest and soundly sleep.

And such the trust that still were mine,
Though stormy winds swept o'er the brine
Or though the tempest's fiery breath
Roused me from sleep to wreck and death
In ocean cave, still safe with Thee
The germ of immortality!
And calm and peaceful shall I sleep,
Rocked in the cradle of the deep.

12 september

A September Night
George Marion McClellan (1860–1934)

The full September moon sheds floods of light,
And all the bayou's face is gemmed with stars,
Save where are dropped fantastic shadows down
From sycamores and moss-hung cypress trees.
With slumberous sound the waters half asleep
Creep on and on their way, 'twixt rankish reeds,
Through marsh and lowlands stretching to the Gulf.
Begirt with cotton fields, Anguilla sits
Half bird-like, dreaming on her Summer nest.
Amid her spreading figs and roses, still
In bloom with all their Spring and Summer hues,
Pomegranates hang with dapple cheeks full ripe,
And over all the town a dreamy haze
Drops down. The great plantations, stretching far
Away, are plains of cotton, downy white.
O, glorious is this night of joyous sounds;
Too full for sleep. Aromas wild and sweet,
From muscadine, late blooming jessamine,
And roses, all the heavy air suffuse.
Faint bellows from the alligators come
From swamps afar, where sluggish lagoons give
To them a peaceful home. The katydids
Make ceaseless cries. Ten thousand insects' wings
Stir in the moonlight haze and joyous shouts
Of Negro song and mirth awake hard by
The cabin dance. O, glorious is this night!
The Summer sweetness fills my heart with songs
I can not sing, with loves I can not speak.

13 september

Evenen in the Village
William Barnes (1801–1886)

Now the light o' the west is a-turn'd to gloom,
An' the men be at hwome vrom ground;
An' the bells be a-zenden all down the Coombe
From tower, their mwoansome sound.
An' the wind is still,
An' the house-dogs do bark,
An' the rooks be a-vled to the elems high an' dark,
An' the water do roar at mill.

An' the flickeren light drough the window-peane
Vrom the candle's dull fleame do shoot,
An' young Jemmy the smith is a-gone down leane
A-playen his shrill-vaiced flute.
An' the miller's man
Do zit down at his ease
On the seat that is under the cluster o' trees,
Wi' his pipe an' his cider can.

14 september

Elegy Written in a Country Churchyard (extract)
Thomas Gray (1716-1771)

The curfew tolls the knell of parting day,
   The lowing herd wind slowly o'er the lea,
The plowman homeward plods his weary way,
   And leaves the world to darkness and to me.

Now fades the glimmering landscape on the sight,
   And all the air a solemn stillness holds,
Save where the beetle wheels his droning flight,
   And drowsy tinklings lull the distant folds;

Save that from yonder ivy-mantled tower
   The moping owl does to the moon complain
Of such, as wandering near her secret bower,
   Molest her ancient solitary reign.

15 september

The Old Vicarage, Grantchester (extract)
Rupert Brooke (1887–1915)

   Ah God! to see the branches stir
Across the moon at Granchester!
To smell the thrilling-sweet and rotten
Unforgettable, unforgotten
River-smell, and hear the breeze
Sobbing in the little trees.
Say, do the elm-clumps greatly stand
Still guardians of that holy land?
The chestnuts shade, in reverend dream,
The yet unacademic stream?
Is dawn a secret shy and cold
Anadyomene, silver-gold?
And sunset still a golden sea
From Haslingfield to Madingley?
And after, ere the night is born,
Do hares come out about the corn?
Oh, is the water sweet and cool,
Gentle and brown, above the pool?
And laughs the immortal river still
Under the mill, under the mill?
Say, is the Beauty yet to find?
And Certainty? And Quiet kind?
Deep meadows yet, for to forget
The lies, and truths, and pain? . . . Oh! yet
Stands the Church clock at ten to three?
And is there honey still for tea?

16 september

Lycidas (extract)
John Milton (1608–1674)

Now, Lycidas, the shepherds weep no more;
Henceforth thou art the Genius of the shore,
In thy large recompense, and shalt be good
To all that wander in that perilous flood.

   Thus sang the uncouth swain to the oaks and rills,
While the still morn went out with sandals grey;
He touched the tender stops of various quills,
With eager thought warbling his Doric lay.
And now the sun had stretched out all the hills,
And now was dropped into the western bay;
At last he rose, and twitched his mantle blue:
Tomorrow to fresh woods, and pastures new.

17 september

Wind and Silver
Amy Lowell (1874-1925)

Greatly shining,
The Autumn moon floats in the thin sky;
And the fish ponds shake their backs and flash their dragon scales
As she passes over them.

18 september

'A boat, beneath a sunny sky'
Lewis Carroll (1832–1898)

A boat, beneath a sunny sky,
Lingering onward dreamily
In an evening of July –

Children three that nestle near,
Eager eye and willing ear,
Pleased a simple tale to hear –

Long has paled that sunny sky:
Echoes fade and memories die:
Autumn frosts have slain July.

Still she haunts me, phantomwise,
Alice moving under skies
Never seen by waking eyes.

Children yet, the tale to hear,
Eager eye and willing ear,
Lovingly shall nestle near.

In Wonderland they lie,
Dreaming as the days go by,
Dreaming as the summers die:

Ever drifting down the stream –
Lingering in the golden gleam –
Life, what is it but a dream?

19 september

Pastoral
Peter Didsbury (b. 1946)
(for Ralf Andtbacka, after his Swedish)

A swollen moon is grazing out on the wold.
Deer stand motionless underneath the trees,
cardboard cut-outs, staring, unwieldy.
Where do you linger, my friend? The hour is late,
and already the farmer has taken to his bed. I, though,
I lie awake and wait for you. Through the yard
pads black cat Lucifer with soft deliberate tread.
Steaming cattle stand and dream in the byre. Lofts groan
with meat and bread, berries, polished fruit. Spilt grain
lines the trackway verges with gold. And all things
are content, all are at rest, sing their small still song
of contentment, and of rest.

20 september

The Fort of Rathangan
***Anonymous, translated from Irish
by Kuno Meyer (1858–1919)***

The fort over against the oak-wood,
Once it was Bruidge's, it was Cathal's,
It was Aed's, it was Ailill's,
It was Conaing's, it was Cuiline's,
And it was Maelduin's;
The fort remains after each in his turn –
And the kings asleep in the ground.

21 september

The Swan
John Gould Fletcher (1886–1950)

Under a wall of bronze,
Where beeches dip and trail
Their branches in the water;
With red-tipped head and wings –
A beaked ship under sail –
There glides a single swan.

Under the autumn trees
He goes. The branches quiver,
Dance in the wraith-like water,
Which ripples beneath the sedge
With the slackening furrow that glides
In his wake when he is gone:
The beeches bow dark heads.

Into the windless dusk,
Where in mist great towers stand
Guarding a lonely strand,
That is bodiless and dim,
He speeds with easy stride;
And I would go beside,
Till the low brown hills divide
At last, for me and him.

22 september

Autumn Birds
John Clare (1793–1864)

The wild duck startles like a sudden thought
And heron slow as if it might be caught.
The flopping crows on weary wings go by
And grey beard jackdaws noising as they fly.
The crowds of starnels wiz and hurry by
And darken like a cloud the evening sky.
The larks like thunder rise and study round
Then drop and nestle in the stubble ground.
The wild swan hurries high and noises loud
With white necks peering to the evening cloud.
The weary rooks to distant woods are gone;
With length of tail the magpie winnows on
To neighbouring tree and leaves the distant crow
While small birds nestle in the hedge below.

23 september

Modern Love (extract)
George Meredith (1828-1909)

We saw the swallows gathering in the sky,
And in the osier-isle we heard them noise.
We had not to look back on summer joys,
Or forward to a summer of bright dye.
But in the largeness of the evening earth
Our spirits grew as we went side by side.
The hour became her husband and my bride.
Love that had robbed us so, thus blessed our dearth!
The pilgrims of the year wax'd very loud
In multitudinous chatterings, as the flood
Full brown came from the West, and like pale blood
Expanded to the upper crimson cloud.
Love that had robbed us of immortal things,
This little moment mercifully gave,
Where I have seen across the twilight wave
The swan sail with her young beneath her wings.

24 september

Canticle
John F. Deane (b. 1943)

Sometimes when you walk down to the red gate
hearing the scrape-music of your shoes across gravel,
a yellow moon will lift over the hill;
you swing the gate shut and lean on the topmost bar
as if something has been accomplished in the world;
a night wind mistles through the poplar leaves
and all the noise of the universe stills
to an oboe hum, the given note of a perfect
music; there is a vast sky wholly dedicated
to the stars and you know, with certainty,
that all the dead are out, up there, in one
holiday flotilla, and that they celebrate
the fact of a red gate and a yellow moon
that tunes their instruments with you to the symphony.

25 september

Roads
Amy Lowell (1874-1925)

I know a country laced with roads,
They join the hills and they span the brooks,
They weave like a shuttle between broad fields,
And slide discreetly through hidden nooks.
They are canopied like a Persian dome
And carpeted with orient dyes.
They are myriad-voiced, and musical,
And scented with happiest memories.
O Winding roads that I know so well,
Every twist and turn, every hollow and hill!
They are set in my heart to a pulsing tune
Gay as a honey-bee humming in June.
'Tis the rhythmic beat of a horse's feet
And the pattering paws of a sheep-dog bitch;
'Tis the creaking trees, and the singing breeze,
And the rustle of leaves in the road-side ditch.

A cow in a meadow shakes her bell
And the notes cut sharp through the autumn air,
Each chattering brook bears a fleet of leaves
Their cargo the rainbow, and just now where
The sun splashed bright on the road ahead
A startled rabbit quivered and fled.
O Uphill roads and roads that dip down!
You curl your sun-spattered length along,
And your march is beaten into a song
By the softly ringing hoofs of a horse
And the panting breath of the dogs I love.
The pageant of Autumn follows its course
And the blue sky of Autumn laughs above.

And the song and the country become as one,
I see it as music, I hear it as light;
Prismatic and shimmering, trembling to tone,
The land of desire, my soul's delight.
And always it beats in my listening ears
With the gentle thud of a horse's stride,
With the swift-falling steps of many dogs,
Following, following at my side.
O Roads that journey to fairyland!
Radiant highways whose vistas gleam,
Leading me on, under crimson leaves,
To the opaline gates of the Castles of Dream.

26 september

Dog
Harold Monro (1879-1932)

You little friend, your nose is ready; you sniff,
Asking for that expected walk,
(Your nostrils full of the happy rabbit-whiff)
And almost talk.

And so the moment becomes a moving force;
Coats glide down from their pegs in the humble dark;
The sticks grow live to the stride of their vagrant course.
You scamper the stairs,
Your body informed with the scent and the track and the mark
Of stoats and weasels, moles and badgers and hares.

We are going OUT. You know the pitch of the word,
Probing the tone of thought as it comes through fog
And reaches by devious means (half-smelt, half-heard)
The four-legged brain of a walk-ecstatic dog.

Out in the garden your head is already low.
(Can you smell the rose? Ah, no.)
But your limbs can draw
Life from the earth through the touch of your padded paw.

Now, sending a little look to us behind,
Who follow slowly the track of your lovely play,
You carry our bodies forward away from mind
Into the light and fun of your useless day.

Thus, for your walk, we took ourselves, and went
Out by the hedge and the tree to the open ground.
You ran, in delightful strata of wafted scent,
Over the hill without seeing the view;
Beauty is smell upon primitive smell to you:
To you, as to us, it is distant and rarely found.

Home ... and further joy will be surely there:
Supper waiting full of the taste of bone.
You throw up your nose again, and sniff, and stare
For the rapture known

Of the quick wild gorge of food and the still lie-down
While your people talk above you in the light
Of candles, and your dreams will merge and drown
Into the bed-delicious hours of night.

27 september

Camomile Tea
Katherine Mansfield (1888-1923)

Outside the sky is light with stars
There's a hollow roaring from the sea
And alas for the little almond flowers!
The wind is shaking the almond tree.

How little I thought a year ago
In that horrible cottage upon the Lee
That Bogey and I should be sitting so
And sipping a cup of camomile tea.

Light as feathers the witches fly
The horn of the moon is plain to see.
By a firefly under a jonquil flower
A goblin is toasting a bumble-bee.

We might be fifty we might be five
So snug so compact so wise are we!
Under the kitchen table leg
My knee is pressing against Jack's knee.

But our shutters are shut the fire is low
The tap is dripping peacefully
The saucepan shadows on the wall
Are black and round and plain to see.

28 september

Moonlit Apples
John Drinkwater (1882–1937)

At the top of the house the apples are laid in rows,
And the skylight lets the moonlight in, and those
Apples are deep-sea apples of green. There goes
   A cloud on the moon in the autumn night.

A mouse in the wainscot scratches, and scratches, and then
There is no sound at the top of the house of men
Or mice; and the cloud is blown, and the moon again
   Dapples the apples with deep-sea light.

They are lying in rows there, under the gloomy beams;
On the sagging floor; they gather the silver streams
Out of the moon, those moonlit apples of dreams,
   And quiet is the steep stair under.

In the corridors under there is nothing but sleep.
And stiller than ever on orchard boughs they keep
Tryst with the moon, and deep is the silence, deep
   On moon-washed apples of wonder.

29 september

'Wynken, Blynken, and Nod'
Eugene Field (1850–1895)

Wynken, Blynken, and Nod one night
   Sailed off in a wooden shoe, –
Sailed on a river of crystal light
   Into a sea of dew.
'Where are you going, and what do you wish?'
     The old moon asked the three.
'We have come to fish for the herring-fish
   That live in this beautiful sea;
   Nets of silver and gold have we',
       Said Wynken,
       Blynken,
       And Nod.

The old moon laughed and sang a song,
   As they rocked in the wooden shoe;
And the wind that sped them all night long
   Ruffled the waves of dew;
The little stars were the herring-fish
   That lived in the beautiful sea.
'Now cast your nets wherever you wish, –
   Never afraid are we!'
   So cried the stars to the fishermen three,
       Wynken,
       Blynken,
       And Nod.

All night long their nets they threw
    To the stars in the twinkling foam, –
Then down from the skies came the wooden shoe,
    Bringing the fishermen home:
'Twas all so pretty a sail, it seemed
    As if it could not be;
And some folk thought 'twas a dream they'd dreamed
    Of sailing that beautiful sea;
    But I shall name you the fishermen three:
        Wynken,
        Blynken,
        And Nod.

Wynken and Blynken are two little eyes,
    And Nod is a little head,
And the wooden shoe that sailed the skies
    Is a wee one's trundle-bed;
So shut your eyes while Mother sings
    Of wonderful sights that be,
And you shall see the beautiful things
    As you rock in the misty sea
    Where the old shoe rocked the fishermen three: –
        Wynken,
        Blynken,
        And Nod.

30 september

The House of Sleep (extract from
Confessio Amantis)
John Gower (c. 1330-1408)

Under an hill there is a Cave.
Which of the Sun may not have,
So that no man may know aright
The point between the day and night:
There is no fire, there is no spark,
There is no door, which may chark,
Whereof an eye should unshut,
So that inward there is no let.
And for to speak of that without,
There stands no great Tree nigh about
Whereon there might crow or pie
Alight, for to clepe or cry;
There is no cock to crow day,
Nor beast none which noise may
The hill, but all about round
There is growing upon the ground
Poppy, which bears the seed of sleep,
With other herbs such a heap.
A still water for the nones
Running upon the small stones,
Which hight of Lethes the river,
Under that hell in such manner
There is, which gives great appetite
To sleep. And thus full of delight
Sleep hath his house; and of his couche
Within his chamber if I shall touch,

Of ebony that Sleepy Tree
The boards all about be,
And for he should sleepe soft;
Upon a featherbed aloft
He lieth with many a pillow of down:
The chamber is strowed up and down
With swevens many thousandfold.

october

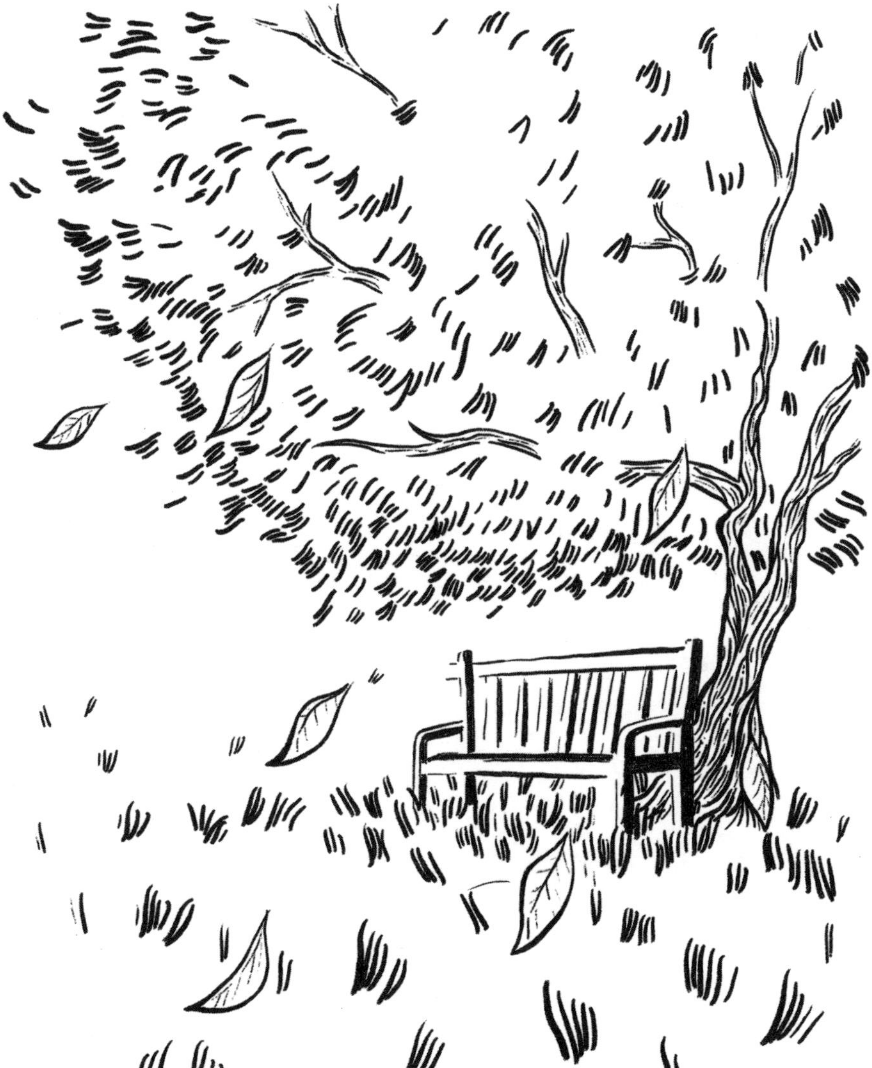

1 october

Evensong
Ridgeley Torrence (1874-1950)

Beauty calls and gives no warning,
Shadows rise and wander on the day.
In the twilight, in the quiet evening,
We shall rise and smile and go away.
Over the flaming leaves
Freezes the sky.
It is the season grieves,
Not you, not I.
All our spring-times, all our summers,
We have kept the longing warm within.
Now we leave the after-comers
To attain the dreams we did not win.
O we have wakened, Sweet, and had our birth,
And that's the end of earth;
And we have toiled and smiled and kept the light,
And that's the end of night.

2 october

Dejection: An Ode
Samuel Taylor Coleridge (1772-1834)

'Tis midnight, but small thoughts have I of sleep:
Full seldom may my friend such vigils keep!
Visit her, gentle Sleep! with wings of healing,
     And may this storm be but a mountain-birth,
May all the stars hang bright above her dwelling,
     Silent as though they watched the sleeping
     Earth!
        With light heart may she rise,
        Gay fancy, cheerful eyes,
   Joy lift her spirit, joy attune her voice;
To her may all things live, from pole to pole,
Their life the eddying of her living soul!
     O simple spirit, guided from above,
Dear Lady! friend devoutest of my choice,
Thus mayest thou ever, evermore rejoice.

3 october

To Autumn
John Keats (1795–1821)

Season of mists and mellow fruitfulness,
   Close bosom-friend of the maturing sun;
Conspiring with him how to load and bless
   With fruit the vines that round the thatch-eaves run;
To bend with apples the mossed cottage-trees,
   And fill all fruit with ripeness to the core;
     To swell the gourd, and plump the hazel shells
   With a sweet kernel; to set budding more,
And still more, later flowers for the bees,
Until they think warm days will never cease,
     For Summer has o'er-brimmed their clammy cells.

Who hath not seen thee oft amid thy store?
   Sometimes whoever seeks abroad may find
Thee sitting careless on a granary floor,
   Thy hair soft-lifted by the winnowing wind;
Or on a half-reaped furrow sound asleep,
   Drowsed with the fume of poppies, while thy hook
     Spares the next swath and all its twinèd flowers:
And sometimes like a gleaner thou dost keep
   Steady thy laden head across a brook;
   Or by a cider-press, with patient look,
     Thou watchest the last oozings hours by hours.

Where are the songs of Spring? Aye, where are they?
    Think not of them, thou hast thy music too –
While barrèd clouds bloom the soft-dying day,
    And touch the stubble-plains with rosy hue;
Then in a wailful choir the small gnats mourn
    Among the river sallows, borne aloft
        Or sinking as the light wind lives or dies;
And full-grown lambs loud bleat from hilly bourn;
    Hedge crickets sing; and now with treble soft
The redbreast whistles from a garden-croft;
    And gathering swallows twitter in the skies.

4 october

Autumn
T. E. Hulme (1883–1917)

A touch of cold in the Autumn night –
I walked abroad,
And saw the ruddy moon lean over a hedge
Like a red-faced farmer.
I did not stop to speak, but nodded,
And round about were the wistful stars
With white faces like town children.

5 october

Milk for the Cat
Harold Monro (1879–1932)

When the tea is brought at five o'clock,
And all the neat curtains are drawn with care,
The little black cat with bright green eyes
Is suddenly purring there.

At first she pretends, having nothing to do,
She has come in merely to blink by the grate,
But, though tea may be late or the milk may be sour,
She is never late.

And presently her agate eyes
Take a soft large milky haze,
And her independent casual glance
Becomes a stiff hard gaze.

Then she stamps her claws or lifts her ears,
Or twists her tail and begins to stir,
Till suddenly all her lithe body becomes
One breathing trembling purr.

The children eat and wriggle and laugh;
The two old ladies stroke their silk;
But the cat is grown small and thin with desire,
Transformed to a creeping lust for milk.

[cont.]

The white saucer like some full moon descends
At last from the clouds of the table above;
She sighs and dreams and thrills and glows,
Transfigured with love.

She nestles over the shining rim,
Buries her chin in the creamy sea;
Her tail hangs loose; each drowsy paw
Is doubled under each bending knee.

A long dim ecstasy holds her life;
Her world is an infinite shapeless white,
Till her tongue has curled the last holy drop,
Then she sinks back into the night,

Draws and dips her body to heap
Her sleepy nerves in the great arm-chair,
Lies defeated and buried deep
Three or four hours unconscious there.

6 october

The Fog
Lola Ridge (1873-1941)

Out of the lamp-bestarred and clouded dusk
Snaring, illuding, concealing,
Magically conjuring
Turning to fairy-coaches
Beetle-backed limousines
Scampering under the great Arch
Making a decoy of blue overalls
And mystery of a scarlet shawl
Indolently –
Knowing no impediment of its sure advance –
Descends the fog.

7 october

Audides
**Henri Thomas, translated from the French
by Jennie Feldman and Stephen Romer**

How I loved you, slowness,
the soul's cautious winding through life
which is mountain, which is cloud, which is
dense smoke, shadowy bakery,
cattle going home to farms, dogs barking,
blackness of barns, lamp roaming
as it's swung in the hay under cobwebs:
the soul likewise radiant
being intimate with evening ...
Morning signalled by the anvil, the wheel,
pigeons outside the shutters, the wisp of sadness
fading in the presence of hills summoned to my window
so that I can admire, can adore
this world lofted into the colour blue,
– O landscape, you weren't so sure,
O memory, jilted city,
what I breathe is no longer the wind that brought you
the scent of evening, morning's freshness,
and breezes that swirl down powdery lanes,
rolling the feel of forests, enlivening
all that drowsed in my afternoon,
O city who never shut yourself off from the tide
of seasons, who drank long draughts of home,
now a dead city where my poem is alone
with the star and the ungraspable spirit
that hurls its fires, transfixing
the soul forever drunk with life.

8 october

Philip and Mildred
Adelaide Anne Procter (1825-1864)

Lingering fade the rays of daylight, and the listening air is chilly;
    Voice of bird and forest murmur, insect hum and quivering spray,
Stir not in that quiet hour: through the valley, calm and stilly,
    All in hushed and loving silence watch the slow departing Day.

9 october

Written Near a Port on a Dark Evening
Charlotte Smith (1749-1806)

Huge vapours brood above the clifted shore,
Night on the ocean settles, dark and mute,
Save where is heard the repercussive roar
Of drowsy billows, on the rugged foot
Of rocks remote; or still more distant tone
Of seamen in the anchored bark that tell
The watch relieved; or one deep voice alone
Singing the hour, and bidding 'Strike the bell.'
All is black shadow, but the lucid line
Marked by the light surf on the level sand,
Or where afar the ship-lights faintly shine
Like wandering fairy fires, that oft on land
Mislead the pilgrim – such the dubious ray
That wavering reason lends, in life's long darkling way.

10 october

Hunter's Moon
Moya Cannon (b. 1956)

There are perhaps no accidents,
no coincidences.
When we stumble against people, books, rare moments out of time,
these are illuminations –
like the hunter's moon that sails tonight in its high clouds,
casting light into our black harbour,
where four black turf boats
tug at their ropes,
hunger for the islands.

11 october

Autumn River Song: On the Broad Reach
Li T'ai Po (701–762), translated by Amy Lowell (1874–1925)

In the clear green water – the shimmering moon.
In the moonlight – white herons flying.
A young man hears a girl plucking water-chestnuts;
They paddle home together through the night, singing.

12 october

'O come with me'
Emily Brontë (1818–1848)

O come with me, thus ran the song,
The moon is bright in Autumn's sky,
And thou hast toiled and laboured long,
With aching head and weary eye.

13 october

Tonight of Yesterday
Vona Groarke (b. 1964)

The evening slips you into it, has kept a place for you
and those wildwood limbs that have already settled on
the morning. The words you have for it are flyblown now
as the dandelion you'll whistle tomorrow into a lighter air.
But tonight, your sleep will be as round as your mouth,
berried with the story of sunlight finally run to ground.
You are all about tomorrow. The moon has your name
memorised: the curl of your back, your face, an open book.

14 october

Evening Quatrains
Charles Cotton (1630–1687)

The Day's grown old, the fainting Sun
Has but a little way to run,
And yet his Steeds, with all his skill,
Scarce lug the Chariot down the Hill.

With Labour spent, and Thirst opprest,
Whilst they strain hard to gain the West,
From Fetlocks hot drops melted light,
Which turn to Meteors in the Night.

The Shadows now so long do grow,
That Brambles like tall Cedars show,
Mole-hills seem Mountains, and the Ant
Appears a monstrous Elephant.

A very little little Flock
Shades thrice the ground that it would stock;
Whilst the small Stripling following them,
Appears a mighty *Polypheme*.

These being brought into the Fold,
And by the thrifty Master told,
He thinks his Wages are well paid,
Since none are either lost, or stray'd.

[cont.]

Now lowing Herds are each-where heard,
Chains rattle in the Villeins Yard,
The Cart's on Tayl set down to rest,
Bearing on high the Cuckolds Crest.

The hedg is stript, the Clothes brought in,
Nought's left without should be within,
The Bees are hiv'd, and hum their Charm,
Whilst every House does seem a Swarm.

The Cock now to the Roost is prest:
For he must call up all the rest;
The Sow's fast pegg'd within the Sty,
To still her squeaking Progeny.

Each one has had his Supping Mess,
The Cheese is put into the Press,
The Pans and Bowls clean scalded all,
Rear'd up against the Milk-house Wall.

And now on Benches all are sat
In the cool Air to sit and chat,
Till *Phoebus*, dipping in the West,
Shall lead the World the way to Rest.

15 october

Interim
Lola Ridge (1873–1941)

The earth is motionless
And poised in space . . .
A great bird resting in its flight
Between the alleys of the stars.
It is the wind's hour off . . .
The wind has nestled down among the corn . . .
The two speak privately together,
Awaiting the whirr of wings.

16 october

Autumn
Amy Lowell *(1874-1925)*

All day I have watched the purple vine leaves
Fall into the water.
And now in the moonlight they still fall,
But each leaf is fringed with silver.

17 october

'Western wind, when wilt thou blow?'
Anonymous

Western wind, when wilt thou blow,
The small rain down can rain?
Christ, if my love were in my arms,
And I in my bed again.

18 october

On the Eclipse of the Moon, October 1865
Charles Tennyson Turner (1808-1879)

One little noise of life remain'd – I heard
The train pause in the distance, then rush by,
Brawling and hushing, like some busy fly
That murmurs and then settles; nothing stirr'd
Beside. The shadow of our travelling earth
Hung on the silver moon, which mutely went
Through that grand process, without token sent,
Or any sign to call a gazer forth,
Had I not chanced to see; dumb was the vault
Of heaven, and dumb the fields – no zephyr swept
The forest walks, or through the coppice crept;
Nor other sound the stillness did assault,
Save that faint-brawling railway's move and halt;
So perfect was the silence Nature kept.

19 october

Ulysses and the Siren (extract)
Samuel Daniel (1562-1619)

SIREN. Come, worthy Greek, Ulysses, come,
Possess these shores with me;
The winds and seas are troublesome,
And here we may be free.
Here may we sit and view their toil
That travail in the deep,
And joy the day in mirth the while,
And spend the night in sleep.

20 october

'Blazing in gold and quenching in purple'
Emily Dickinson (1830–1886)

Blazing in Gold and quenching in Purple
Leaping like Leopards to the Sky
Then at the feet of the old Horizon
Laying her spotted Face to die
Stooping as low as the Otter's Window
Touching the Roof and tinting the Barn
Kissing her Bonnet to the Meadow
And the Juggler of Day is gone.

21 october

Silver
Walter de la Mare (1873–1956)

Slowly, silently, now the moon
Walks the night in her silver shoon;
This way, and that, she peers, and sees
Silver fruit upon silver trees;
One by one the casements catch
Her beams beneath the silvery thatch;
Couched in his kennel, like a log,
With paws of silver sleeps the dog;
From their shadowy cote the white breasts peep
Of doves in a silver-feathered sleep;
A harvest mouse goes scampering by,
With silver claws, and silver eye;
And moveless fish in the water gleam,
By silver reeds in a silver stream.

22 october

The Poet and His Song
Paul Laurence Dunbar (1872–1906)

A song is but a little thing,
And yet what joy it is to sing!
In hours of toil it gives me zest,
And when at eve I long for rest;
When cows come home along the bars,
And in the fold I hear the bell,
As Night, the shepherd, herds his stars,
I sing my song, and all is well.

There are no ears to hear my lays,
No lips to lift a word of praise;
But still, with faith unfaltering,
I live and laugh and love and sing.
What matters yon unheeding throng?
They cannot feel my spirit's spell,
Since life is sweet and love is long,
I sing my song, and all is well.

My days are never days of ease;
I till my ground and prune my trees.
When ripened gold is all the plain,
I put my sickle to the grain.
I labour hard, and toil and sweat,
While others dream within the dell;
But even while my brow is wet,
I sing my song, and all is well.

Sometimes the sun, unkindly hot,
My garden makes a desert spot;
Sometimes a blight upon the tree
Takes all my fruit away from me;
And then with throes of bitter pain
Rebellious passions rise and swell;
But – life is more than fruit or grain,
And so I sing, and all is well.

23 october

Lines Composed a Few Miles above Tintern Abbey (extract)
William Wordsworth (1770–1850)

   This prayer I make,
Knowing that Nature never did betray
The heart that loved her; 'tis her privilege,
Through all the years of this our life, to lead
From joy to joy: for she can so inform
The mind that is within us, so impress
With quietness and beauty, and so feed
With lofty thoughts, that neither evil tongues,
Rash judgements, nor the sneers of selfish men,
Nor greetings where no kindness is, nor all
The dreary intercourse of daily life,
Shall e'er prevail against us, or disturb
Our cheerful faith, that all which we behold
Is full of blessings. Therefore let the moon
Shine on thee in thy solitary walk;
And let the misty mountain-winds be free
To blow against thee: and, in after years,
When these wild ecstasies shall be matured
Into a sober pleasure; when thy mind
Shall be a mansion for all lovely forms,
Thy memory be as a dwelling-place
For all sweet sounds and harmonies; oh! then,
If solitude, or fear, or pain, or grief,
Should be thy portion, with what healing thoughts
Of tender joy wilt thou remember me,
And these my exhortations!

24 october

A Ballad of Dreamland
Algernon Charles Swinburne (1837–1909)

I hid my heart in a nest of roses,
   Out of the sun's way, hidden apart;
In a softer bed than the soft white snow's is,
   Under the roses I hid my heart.
   Why would it sleep not? why should it start,
When never a leaf of the rose-tree stirred?
   What made sleep flutter his wings and part?
Only the song of a secret bird.

Lie still, I said, for the wind's wing closes,
   And mild leaves muffle the keen sun's dart;
Lie still, for the wind of the warm sea dozes,
   And the wind is unquieter yet than thou art.
   Does a thought in thee still as a thorn's wound smart?
Does the fang still fret thee of hope deferred?
   What bids the lids of thy sleep dispart?
Only the song of a secret bird.

The green land's name that a charm encloses,
   It never was writ in the traveller's chart,
And sweet as the fruit on its tree that grows is,
   It never was sold in the merchant's mart.
   The swallows of dreams through its dim fields dart,
And sleep's are the tunes in its tree tops heard;
   No hound's note wakens the wildwood hart,
Only the song of a secret bird.

25 october

She Walks in Beauty
George Gordon, Lord Byron (1788–1824)

She walks in beauty, like the night
Of cloudless climes and starry skies;
And all that's best of dark and bright
Meet in her aspect and her eyes:
Thus mellowed to that tender light
Which heaven to gaudy day denies.

One shade the more, one ray the less,
Had half impaired the nameless grace
Which waves in every raven tress,
Or softly lightens o'er her face;
Where thoughts serenely sweet express
How pure, how dear their dwelling-place.

And on that cheek, and o'er that brow,
So soft, so calm, yet eloquent,
The smiles that win, the tints that glow,
But tell of days in goodness spent,
A mind at peace with all below,
A heart whose love is innocent!

26 october

To Imagination
Emily Brontë (1818–1848)

When weary with the long day's care,
And earthly change from pain to pain,
And lost, and ready to despair,
Thy kind voice calls me back again –
O my true friend, I am not lone
While thou canst speak with such a tone!

So hopeless is the world without,
The world within I doubly prize;
Thy world where guile and hate and doubt
And cold suspicion never rise;
Where thou and I and Liberty
Have undisputed sovereignty.

What matters it that all around
Danger and grief and darkness lie,
If but within our bosom's bound
We hold a bright unsullied sky,
Warm with ten thousand mingled rays
Of suns that know no winter days?

[cont.]

Reason indeed may oft complain
For Nature's sad reality,
And tell the suffering heart how vain
Its cherished dreams must always be;
And truth may rudely trample down
The flowers of Fancy newly blown.

But thou art ever there to bring
The hovering visions back and breathe
New glories o'er the blighted spring
And call a lovelier life from death,
And whisper with a voice divine
Of real worlds as bright as thine.

I trust not to thy phantom bliss,
Yet still in evening's quiet hour
With never-failing thankfulness
I welcome thee, benignant power,
Sure solacer of human cares
And brighter hope when hope despairs.

27 october

Birch Trees
John Richard Moreland (1878–1947)

The night is white,
   The moon is high,
The birch trees lean
   Against the sky.

The cruel winds
   Have blown away
Each little leaf
   Of silver gray.

O lonely trees
   As white as wool …
That moonlight makes
   So beautiful.

28 october

A Study: At Twilight (extract)
Alice Meynell (1847–1922)

She therefore turned unto the Eastern hills,
Thrilled with a west wind sowing stars. She saw
Her lonely upward way climb to the verge
And ending of the day-time; and she knew
The downward way in presence of the night.
She heard the fitful sheep-bells in the glen
Move like a child's thoughts. There she felt the earth
Lonely in space. And all things suddenly
Shook with her tears. She went with shadowless feet,
Moving along the shadow of the world,
Faring alone to home and a long life,
Setting a twilight face to meet the stars.

29 october

Son-days
Henry Vaughan (1621–1695)

Bright shadows of true rest! some shoots of bliss,
   Heaven once a week;
The next world's gladness prepossessed in this;
   A day to seek
Eternity in time; the steps by which
We climb above all ages; lamps that light
Man through his heap of dark days; and the rich,
And full redemption of the whole week's flight.

The pulleys unto headlong man; time's bower;
   The narrow way;
Transplanted Paradise; God's walking hour;
   The cool o'the day;
The creatures' Jubilee; God's parle with dust;
Heaven here; man on those hills of myrrh, and flowers;
Angels descending; the returns of trust;
A gleam of glory, after six-days-showers.

The Church's love-feasts; time's prerogative,
   And interest
Deducted from the whole; the combs, and hive,
   And home of rest.
The milky way chalked out with suns; a clue
That guides through erring hours; and in full story
A taste of Heaven on earth; the pledge, and cue
Of a full feast; and the out courts of glory.

30 october

Voices of Unseen Spirits
(From *Taliesin: a Masque*)
Richard Hovey (1864–1900)

Here falls no light of sun nor stars;
   No stir nor striving here intrudes;
No moan nor merry-making mars
   The quiet of these solitudes.

Submerged in sleep, the passive soul
   Is one with all the things that seem;
Night blurs in one confusèd whole
   Alike the dreamer and the dream.

O dwellers in the busy town!
   For dreams you smile, for dreams you weep.
Come out, and lay your burdens down!
   Come out; there is no God but Sleep.

Sleep, and renounce the vital day;
   For evil is the child of life.
Let be the will to live, and pray
   To find forgetfulness of strife.

Beneath the thicket of these leaves
  No light discriminates each from each.
No Self that wrongs, no Self that grieves
  Hath longer deed nor creed nor speech.

Sleep on the mighty Mother's breast!
  Sleep, and no more be separate!
Then, one with Nature's ageless rest,
  There shall be no more sin to hate.

31 october

I Am
John Clare (1793–1864)

I am – yet what I am, none cares or knows;
   My friends forsake me like a memory lost: –
I am the self-consumer of my woes; –
   They rise and vanish in oblivion's host,
Like shadows in love's frenzied stifled throes: –
And yet I am, and live – like vapours tost

Into the nothingness of scorn and noise, –
   Into the living sea of waking dreams,
Where there is neither sense of life or joys,
   But the vast shipwreck of my life's esteems;
Even the dearest, that I love the best
Are strange – nay, rather stranger than the rest.

I long for scenes, where man hath never trod
   A place where woman never smiled or wept
There to abide with my Creator, God;
   And sleep as I in childhood, sweetly slept,
Untroubling, and untroubled where I lie,
The grass below – above, the vaulted sky.

november

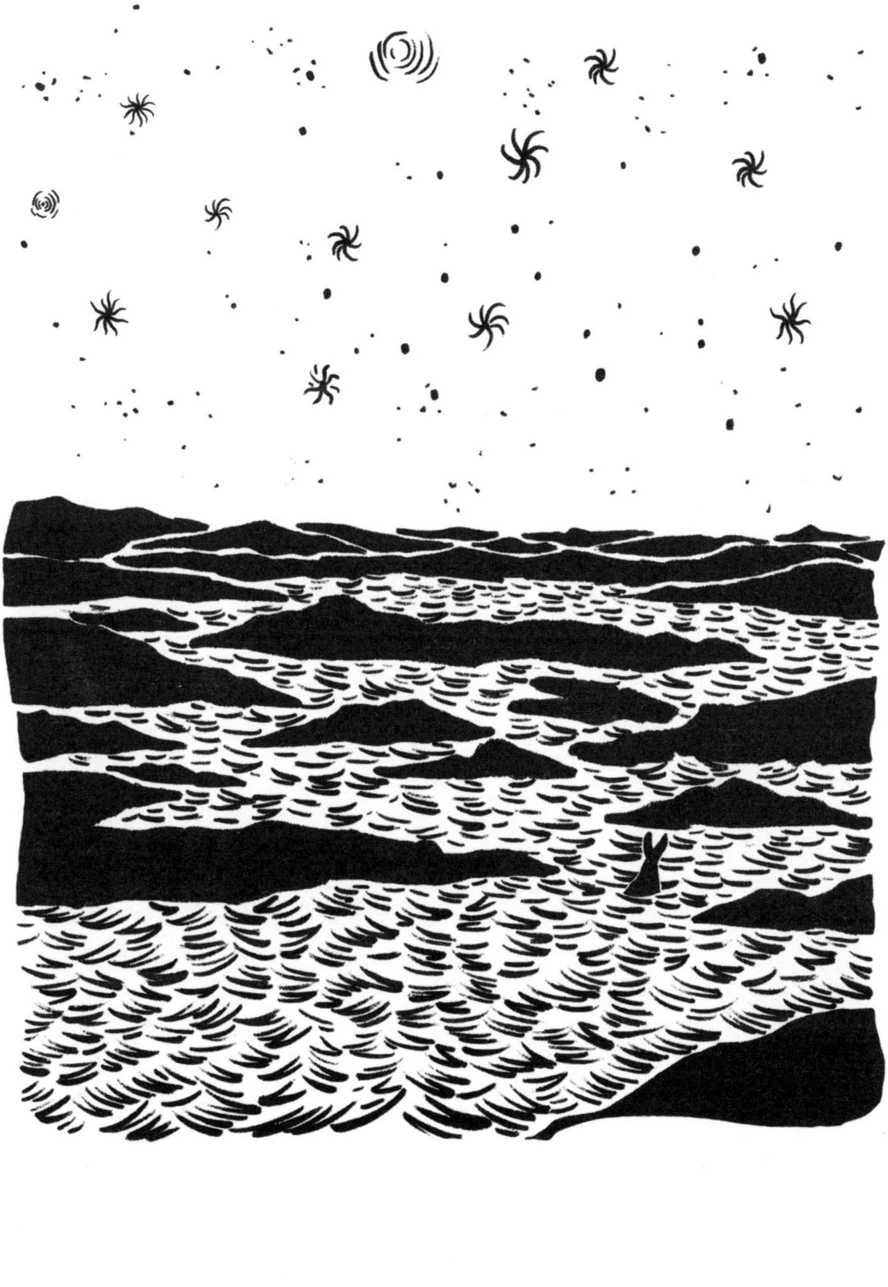

1 november

At the Mid Hour of Night
Thomas Moore (1779–1852)

At the mid hour of night, when stars are weeping, I fly
To the lone vale we loved, when life shone warm in thine eye;
   And I think that if spirits can steal from the regions of air,
    To revisit past scenes of delight, thou wilt come to me there,
And tell me our love is remember'd, even in the sky!

Then I sing the wild song it once was rapture to hear,
When our voices, commingling, breathed, like one, on the ear.
   And, as Echo far off through the vale my sad orison rolls,
    I think, O my love! 'tis thy voice, from the Kingdom of Souls.
Faintly answering still the notes that once were so clear.

2 november

The Starlit Night
Gerard Manley Hopkins (1844–1889)

Look at the stars! look, look up at the skies!
　O look at all the fire-folk sitting in the air!
　The bright boroughs, the circle-citadels there!
Down in dim woods the diamond delves! the elves'-eyes!
The grey lawns cold where gold, where quickgold lies!
　Wind-beat whitebeam! airy abeles set on a flare!
　Flake-doves sent floating forth at a farmyard scare!
Ah well! it is all a purchase, all is a prize.

Buy then! bid then! – What? – Prayer, patience, alms, vows.
Look, look: a May-mess, like on orchard boughs!
　Look! March-bloom, like on mealed-with-yellow sallows!
These are indeed the barn; withindoors house
The shocks. This piece-bright paling shuts the spouse
　Christ home, Christ and his mother and all his hallows.

3 november

Rubric
Josephine Preston Peabody (1874–1922)

I'll not believe the dullard dark,
   Nor all the winds that weep,
But I shall find the farthest dream
   That kisses me, asleep.

4 november

A November Daisy
Henry van Dyke (1852–1933)

Afterthought of summer's bloom!
Late arrival at the feast,
Coming when the songs have ceased
And the merry guests departed,
Leaving but an empty room,
Silence, solitude, and gloom, –
Are you lonely, heavy-hearted;
You, the last of all your kind,
Nodding in the autumn-wind;
Now that all your friends are flown,
Blooming late and all alone?

Nay, I wrong you, little flower,
Reading mournful mood of mine
In your looks, that give no sign
Of a spirit dark and cheerless!
You possess the heavenly power
That rejoices in the hour.
Glad, contented, free, and fearless,
Lift a sunny face to heaven
When a sunny day is given!
Make a summer of your own,
Blooming late and all alone!

[cont.]

Once the daisies gold and white
Sea-like through the meadow rolled:
Once my heart could hardly hold
All its pleasures. I remember,
In the flood of youth's delight
Separate joys were lost to sight.
That was summer! Now November
Sets the perfect flower apart;
Gives each blossom of the heart
Meaning, beauty, grace unknown, –
Blooming late and all alone.

5 november

'Star light, star bright'
Anonymous

Star light, star bright,
First star I see tonight,
I wish I may, I wish I might,
Have this wish I wish tonight.

6 november

The Coming of Good Luck
Robert Herrick (1591–1674)

So Good-Luck came, and on my roof did light,
Like noiseless snow, or as the dew of night;
Not all at once, but gently, – as the trees
Are by the sun-beams, tickled by degrees.

7 november

'Now winter nights enlarge'
Thomas Campion (1567–1620)

Now winter nights enlarge
The number of their hours,
And clouds their storms discharge
Upon the airy towers.
Let now the chimneys blaze,
And cups o'erflow with wine;
Let well-tuned words amaze
With harmony divine.
Now yellow waxen lights
Shall wait on honey Love,
While youthful revels, masks, and courtly sights
Sleep's leaden spells remove.

This time doth well dispense
With lovers' long discourse.
Much speech hath some defence
Though beauty no remorse.
All do not all things well:
Some measures comely tread,
Some knotted riddles tell,
Some poems smoothly read.
The Summer hath his joys,
And Winter his delights.
Though Love and all his pleasures are but toys,
They shorten tedious nights.

8 november

Cat
Lytton Strachey (1880–1932)

Dear creature by the fire a-purr,
    Strange idol, eminently bland,
Miraculous puss! As o'er your fur
    I trail a negligible hand,

And gaze into your gazing eyes,
    And wonder in a demi-dream,
What mystery it is that lies,
    Behind those slits that glare and gleam,

And exquisite enchantment falls
    About the portals of my sense;
Meandering through enormous halls,
    I breathe luxurious frankincense,

An ampler air, a warmer June
    Enfold me, and my wondering eye
Salutes a more imperial moon
    Throned in a more resplendent sky

Than ever knew this northern shore.
    Oh, strange! For you are with me too,
And I who am a cat once more
    Follow the woman that was you

With tail erect and pompous march,
    The proudest puss that ever trod,
Through many a grove, 'neath many an arch,
    Impenetrable as a god.

Down many an alabaster flight
    Of broad and cedar-shaded stairs,
While over us the elaborate night
    Mysteriously gleams and glares.

9 november

Miracles
Walt Whitman (1819–1892)

Why, who makes much of a miracle?
As to me I know of nothing else but miracles,
Whether I walk the streets of Manhattan,
Or dart my sight over the roofs of houses toward the sky,
Or wade with naked feet along the beach just in the edge of the water,
Or stand under trees in the woods,
Or talk by day with any one I love, or sleep in the bed at night with
    any one I love,
Or sit at table at dinner with the rest,
Or look at strangers opposite me riding in the car,
Or watch honey-bees busy around the hive of a summer forenoon,
Or animals feeding in the fields,
Or birds, or the wonderfulness of insects in the air,
Or the wonderfulness of the sundown, or of stars shining so quiet
    and bright,
Or the exquisite delicate thin curve of the new moon in spring;
These with the rest, one and all, are to me miracles,
The whole referring, yet each distinct and in its place.

To me every hour of the light and dark is a miracle,
Every cubic inch of space is a miracle,
Every square yard of the surface of the earth is spread with the same,
Every foot of the interior swarms with the same.

To me the sea is a continual miracle,
The fishes that swim – the rocks – the motion of the waves –
the ships with men in them,
What stranger miracles are there?

10 november

There Remaineth Therefore a Rest for the People of God (extract)
Christina Rossetti (1830–1894)

Come, blessed sleep, most full, most perfect, come:
   Come, sleep, if so I may forget the whole;
   Forget my body and forget my soul,
Forget how long life is and troublesome.
Come, happy sleep, to soothe my heart or numb,
   Arrest my weary spirit or control;
   Till light be dark to me from pole to pole,
And winds and songs and low echoes be dumb,
Come, sleep, and lap me into perfect calm,
   Lap me from all the world and weariness;
Come, secret sleep, with thine unuttered psalm,
   Safe sheltering in a hidden cool recess;
   Come, heavy dreamless sleep, and close and press
Upon mine eyes thy fingers dropping balm.

11 november

Santa Filomena
Henry Wadsworth Longfellow (1807–1882)

Whene'er a noble deed is wrought,
Whene'er is spoken a noble thought,
   Our hearts, in glad surprise,
   To higher levels rise.

The tidal wave of deeper souls
Into our inmost being rolls,
   And lifts us unawares
   Out of all meaner cares.

Honor to those whose words or deeds
Thus help us in our daily needs,
   And by their overflow
   Raise us from what is low!

Thus thought I, as by night I read
Of the great army of the dead,
   The trenches cold and damp,
   The starved and frozen camp, –

The wounded from the battle-plain,
In dreary hospitals of pain,
   The cheerless corridors,
   The cold and stony floors.

Lo! in that house of misery
A lady with a lamp I see
   Pass through the glimmering gloom,
   And flit from room to room.

And slow, as in a dream of bliss,
The speechless sufferer turns to kiss
   Her shadow, as it falls
   Upon the darkening walls.

As if a door in heaven should be
Opened, and then closed suddenly,
   The vision came and went,
   The light shone was spent.

On England's annals, through the long
Hereafter of her speech and song,
   That light its rays shall cast
   From portals of the past.

A Lady with a Lamp shall stand
In the great history of the land,
   A noble type of good,
   Heroic womanhood.

Nor even shall be wanting here
The palm, the lily, and the spear,
   The symbols that of yore
   Saint Filomena bore.

12 november

The Secret Song
Margaret Wise Brown (1910–1952)

Who saw the petals
drop from the rose?
I, said the spider,
But nobody knows.

Who saw the sunset
flash on a bird?
I, said the fish,
But nobody heard.

Who saw the fog
come over the sea?
I, said the sea pigeon,
Only me.

Who saw the first
green light of the sun?
I, said the night owl,
The only one.

Who saw the moss
creep over the stone?
I, said the grey fox,
All alone.

13 november

Thought
D. H. Lawrence (1885–1930)

Thought. I love thought.
But not the jaggling and twisting of already existent ideas
I despise that self-important game.
Thought is the welling up of unknown life into consciousness,
Thought is the testing of statements on the touchstone of conscience,
Thought is gazing on to the face of life, and reading what can be read,
Thought is pondering over experience, and coming to conclusion.
Thought is not a trick, or an exercise, or a set of dodges,
Thought is a man in his wholeness wholly attending.

14 november

Astrophil and Stella: Sonnet 39
Philip Sidney (1554–1586)

Come, Sleep, O Sleep, the certain knot of peace,
  The baiting-place of wit, the balm of woe,
The poor man's wealth, the prisoner's release,
  Th' indifferent judge between the high and low;
With shield of proof shield me from out the press
  Of those fierce darts despair at me doth throw:
O make in me those civil wars to cease;
  I will good tribute pay, if thou do so,
Take thou of me smooth pillows, sweetest bed,
  A chamber deaf to noise and blind to light;
A rosy garland and a weary head:
  And if these things, as being thine by right,
    Move not thy heavy grace, thou shalt in me,
    Livelier than elsewhere, Stella's image see.

15 november

'I dwell in possibility'
Emily Dickinson (1830-1886)

I dwell in Possibility –
A fairer House than Prose –
More numerous of Windows –
Superior – for Doors –

Of chambers as the Cedars –
Impregnable of Eye –
And for an Everlasting Roof
The Gambrels of the Sky –

Of Visitors – the fairest –
For Occupation – This –
The spreading wide my narrow Hands
To gather Paradise –

16 november

A Prayer
St Francis of Assisi (d. 1226)

Lord make me an
   instrument of Thy peace.
   Where there is hatred,
   Let me sow Love;
   Where there is injury,
   Let me sow pardon;
   Where there is doubt, faith;
   Where there is despair, hope;
Where there is darkness, light;
Where there is sadness, joy.
     (Amen)

17 november

Sonnet 318. On His Blindness
John Milton (1608–1674)

When I consider how my light is spent
   Ere half my days, in this dark world and wide,
   And that one Talent which is death to hide,
   Lodg'd with me useless, though my Soul more bent
To serve therewith my Maker, and present
   My true account, least he returning chide,
   Doth God exact day-labour, light deny'd,
   I fondly ask; But patience to prevent
That murmur, soon replies, God doth not need
   Either man's work or his own gifts, who best
   Bear his milde yoak, they serve him best, his State
Is Kingly. Thousands at his bidding speed
   And post o're Land and Ocean without rest:
   They also serve who only stand and waite.

18 november

Twenty Gallons of Sleep
Agnes L. Storrie (1865-1936)

Measure me out from the fathomless tun
    That somewhere or other you keep
In your vasty cellars, O wealthy one,
    Twenty gallons of sleep.

Twenty gallons of balmy sleep,
    Dreamless, and deep, and mild,
Of the excellent brand you used to keep
    When I was a little child.

I've tasted of all your vaunted stock,
    Your clarets and ports of Spain,
The liquid gold of your famous hock,
    And your matchless dry champagne.

Of your rich muscats and your sherries fine,
    I've drunk both well and deep;
Then measure me out, O merchant mine,
    Twenty gallons of sleep.

Twenty gallons of slumber soft,
    Of the innocent, baby kind,
When the angels flutter their wings aloft
    And the pillow with down is lined.

I have drawn the corks, and drained the lees,
    Of every vintage pressed;
If I've felt the sting of my honey bees,
    I've taken it with the rest.

I have lived my life, and I'll not repine;
    As I sowed I was bound to reap;
Then measure me out, O merchant mine,
    Twenty gallons of sleep.

19 november

The Mermaidens' Vesper-Hymn
George Darley (1795–1846)

Troop home to silent grots and caves!
Troop home! and mimic as you go
The mournful winding of the waves
Which to their dark abysses flow!

At this sweet hour, all things beside
In amorous pairs to covert creep;
The swans that brush the evening tide
Homeward in snowy couples keep;

In his green den the murmuring seal
Close by his sleek companion lies;
While singly we to bedward steal,
And close in fruitless sleep our eyes.

In bowers of love men take their rest,
In loveless bowers we sigh alone!
With bosom-friends are others blest, –
But we have none! But we have none!

20 november

To Evening
William Collins (1721–1759)

If aught of oaten stop or pastoral song
May hope, chaste Eve, to soothe thy modest ear
   Like thy own solemn springs,
   Thy springs, and dying gales;

O Nymph reserved, –while now the bright-hair'd sun
Sits in yon western tent, whose cloudy skirts
   With brede ethereal wove,
   O'erhang his wavy bed,

Now air is hush'd, save where the weak-eyed bat
With short shrill shriek flits by on leathern wing,
   Or where the beetle winds
   His small but sullen horn,

As oft he rises midst the twilight path,
Against the pilgrim borne in heedless hum, –
   Now teach me, maid composed,
   To breathe some soften'd strain

Whose numbers, stealing through thy dark'ning vale,
May not unseemly with its stillness suit;
   As musing slow I hail
   Thy genial loved return.

[cont.]

For when thy folding-star arising shows
His paly circlet, at his warning lamp
   The fragrant Hours, and Elves
   Who slept in buds the day,

And many a Nymph who wreathes her brows with sedge
And sheds the freshening dew, and lovelier still
   The pensive Pleasures sweet,
   Prepare thy shadowy car.

Then let me rove some wild and healthy scene;
Or find some ruin midst its dreary dells,
   Whose walls more awful nod
   By thy religious gleams.

Or if chill blustering winds or driving rain
Prevent my willing feet, be mine the hut
   That, from the mountain's side,
   Views wilds and swelling floods,

And hamlets brown, and dim-discover'd spires;
And hears their simple bell; and marks o'er all
   Thy dewy fingers draw
   The gradual dusky veil.

While Spring shall pour his showers, as oft he wont,
And bathe thy breathing tresses, meekest Eve!
   While Summer loves to sport
   Beneath thy lingering light;

While sallow Autumn fills thy lap with leaves;
Or Winter, yelling through the troublous air,
   Affrights thy shrinking train
   And rudely rends thy robes;

So long, regardful of thy quiet rule,
Shall Fancy, Friendship, Science, smiling Peace,
   Thy gentlest influence own,
   And love thy favourite name!

21 november

Old Song
Traditional, West Africa

Do not seek too much fame,
but do not seek obscurity.
Be proud,
But do not remind the world of your deeds.
Excel when you must,
but do not excel the world,
Many heroes are not yet born,
many have already died.
To be alive to hear this song is a victory.

22 november

To-Night
Louise Chandler Moulton (1835–1908)

Bend low, O dusky Night,
   And give my spirit rest.
   Hold me to your deep breast,
And put old cares to flight.
Give back the lost delight
   That once my soul possest,
   When Love was loveliest.
Bend low, O dusky Night!

Enfold me in your arms –
   The sole embrace I crave
   Until the embracing grave
Shield me from life's alarms.
I dare your subtlest charms;
   Your deepest spell I brave, –
   O, strong to slay or save,
Enfold me in your arms!

23 november

The Embankment
T. E. Hulme (1883–1917)

(The fantasia of a fallen gentleman on a cold, bitter night)
Once, in finesse of fiddles found I ecstasy,
In a flash of gold heels on the hard pavement.
Now see I
That warmth's the very stuff of poesy.
Oh, God, make small
The old star-eaten blanket of the sky,
That I may fold it round me and in comfort lie.

24 november

To Sleep
John Keats (1795-1821)

O soft embalmer of the still midnight,
   Shutting, with careful fingers and benign,
Our gloom-pleas'd eyes, embower'd from the light,
   Enshaded in forgetfulness divine:
O soothest Sleep! if so it please thee, close
   In midst of this thine hymn my willing eyes,
Or wait the 'Amen', ere thy poppy throws
   Around my bed its lulling charities.
Then save me, or the passed day will shine
Upon my pillow, breeding many woes,–
   Save me from curious Conscience, that still lords
Its strength for darkness, burrowing like a mole;
   Turn the key deftly in the oiled wards,
And seal the hushed Casket of my Soul.

25 november

Character of a Happy Life
Henry Wotton (1568-1639)

How happy is he born and taught
That serveth not another's will;
Whose armour is his honest thought
And simple truth his utmost skill!

Whose passions not his masters are,
Whose soul is still prepared for death,
Not tied unto the world with care
Of public fame, or private breath;

Who envies none that chance doth raise
Or vice; Who never understood
How deepest wounds are given by praise;
Nor rules of state, but rules of good:

Who hath his life from rumours freed,
Whose conscience is his strong retreat;
Whose state can neither flatterers feed,
Nor ruin make accusers great;

Who God doth late and early pray
More of his grace than gifts to lend;
And entertains the harmless day
With a well-chosen book or friend;

– This man is freed from servile bands
Of hope to rise, or fear to fall;
Lord of himself, though not of lands;
And having nothing, yet hath all.

26 november

Safe Sounds
Carol Ann Duffy (b. 1955)

You like safe sounds:
the dogs lapping at their bowls;
the pop of a cork on a bottle of plonk
as your mother cooks;
the *Match of the Day* theme tune
and *Doctor Who-oo-oo*.

          Safe sounds:
your name called, two happy syllables
from the bottom to the top of the house;
your daft ring tone; the low gargle
of hot water in bubbles. Half asleep
in the drifting boat of your bed,
you like to hear the big trees
sound like the sea instead.

27 november

A Summing Up
Charles Mackay (1814–1889)

I have lived and I have loved;
I have waked and I have slept;
I have sung and I have danced;
I have smiled and I have wept;
I have won and wasted treasure;
I have had my fill of pleasure;
And all these things were weariness,
And some of them were dreariness,
And all these things, but two things,
Were emptiness and pain:
And Love – it was the best of them;
And Sleep – worth all the rest of them.

28 november

Imagination
John Davidson (1857-1909)

There is a dish to hold the sea,
   A brazier to contain the sun,
A compass for the galaxy,
   A voice to wake the dead and done!

That minister of ministers,
   Imagination, gathers up
The undiscovered Universe,
   Like jewels in a jasper cup.

Its flame can mingle north and south;
   Its accent with the thunder strive;
The ruddy sentence of its mouth
   Can make the ancient dead alive.

The mart of power, the fount of will,
   The form and mould of every star,
The source and bound of good and ill,
   The key of all the things that are,

Imagination, new and strange
   In every age, can turn the year;
Can shift the poles and lightly change
   The mood of men, the world's career.

29 november

The Winds of Fate
Ella Wheeler Wilcox (1850-1919)

One ship drives east and another drives west
   With the selfsame winds that blow.
     'Tis the set of the sails
     And not of the gales
   Which tells us the way to go.

Like the winds of the sea are the ways of fate,
   As we voyage along through life;
     'Tis the set of a soul
     That decides its goal,
   And not the calm or strife.

30 november

The Pleasant Dark
Annette Wynne (active 1919-1922)

The pleasant dark that comes at night
Is just as friendly as the light.
Dark wraps a curtain over all –
The trees, the houses, far and tall;
The pleasant dark comes down to bless
The world with mother-tenderness.
She folds her children in her arms
And keeps them safe from loud alarms;
The far green hills where children play
Are hidden till the brand-new day.
For hills and eyelids know what's best –
That darkness-time is time for rest.
The pleasant dark that comes at night
Is just as friendly as the light.

december

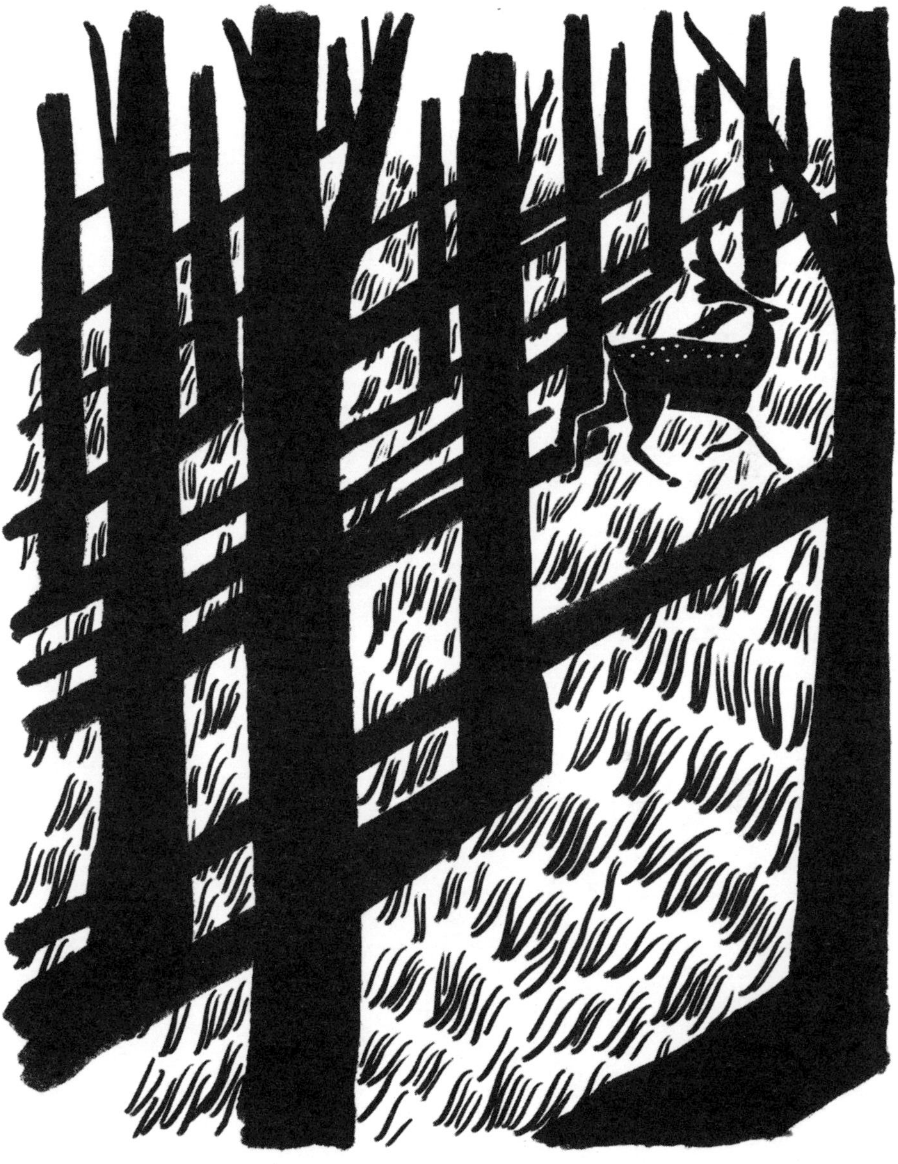

1 december

Hamlet Act 1, Scene 1 (extract)
William Shakespeare (c. 1564–1616)

Some say that ever 'gainst that season comes
Wherein our Saviour's birth is celebrated,
The bird of dawning singeth all night long.
And then, they say, no spirit dares stir abroad;
The nights are wholesome; then no planets strike;
No fairy takes; nor witch hath power to charm,
So hallowed and so gracious is that time.

2 december

'I heard a bird sing'
Oliver Herford (1860–1935)

I heard a bird sing
In the dark of December
A magical thing
And sweet to remember.

'We are nearer to spring
Than we were in September,'
I heard a bird sing
In the dark of December.

3 december

The Chronicles of Narnia
Clare Shaw (b. 1972)

Somewhere, there's another world
behind a door you've been knocking on
since you were young.

It's not that you want to escape your life –
just that somewhere, very close by,
in a room you've never explored,

there's a forest where snow falls
in the warm light cast by a lamp.
The moon hangs in a clear Northern sky,

the stream is frozen.
There are thousands and thousands of stars.
You don't need a key, or a ring

and there's no point in knocking:
every heart is a secret door.
One day, you'll walk right through

and you'll be there.
Perhaps a shadow in the trees will approach you.
You'll feel powerful and brave and very small.

Then your heart will be lion and mountains,
an acre of blue flowers blooming
and you'll stride into a world

you've always believed in
because there was always a river
and bright moss and birdsong

and stars – oh my love
though I didn't know how to reach you
all my life, I knew you were there.

4 december

The Bells (extract)
Edgar Allan Poe *(1809-1849)*

    Hear the sledges with the bells –
        Silver bells!
What a world of merriment their melody foretells!
    How they tinkle, tinkle, tinkle,
      In the icy air of night!
    While the stars that oversprinkle
    All the Heavens, seem to twinkle
      With a crystalline delight;
    Keeping time, time, time,
    In a sort of Runic rhyme,
To the tintinnabulation that so musically wells
   From the bells, bells, bells, bells
      Bells, bells, bells –
  From the jingling and the tinkling of the bells.

        Hear the mellow wedding bells –
                Golden bells!
What a world of happiness their harmony foretells!
        Through the balmy air of night
        How they ring out their delight! –
            From the molten-golden notes,
                And all in tune,
            What a liquid ditty floats
    To the turtle-dove that listens, while she gloats
                On the moon!
        Oh, from out the sounding cells,
What a gush of euphony voluminously wells!
                How it swells!
                How it dwells
            On the Future! – how it tells
            Of the rapture that impels
            To the swinging and the ringing
                Of the bells, bells, bells! –
            Of the bells, bells, bells, bells,
                Bells, bells, bells –
    To the rhyming and chiming of the bells!

5 *december*

Winter
Gerard Manley Hopkins (1844–1889)

The boughs, the boughs are bare enough
But earth has never felt the snow.
Frost-furred our ivies are, and rough

With bills of rime the brambles shew.
The hoarse leaves crawl on hissing ground
Because the sighing wind is low.

But if the rain-blasts be unbound
And from dank feathers wring the drops
The clogged brook runs with choking sound

Kneading the mounded mire that stops
His channel under damming coats
Of foliage fallen in the copse.

A simple passage of weak notes
Is all the winter bird dare try
The bugle moon by daylight floats

So glassy white about the sky,
So like a berg of hyaline,
And pencilled blue so daintily,

I never saw her so divine
But through black branches, rarely drest
In scarves of silky shot and shine.

The webbèd and the watery west
Where yonder crimson fireball sits
Looks laid for feasting and for rest.

I see long reefs of violets
In beryl-covered fens so dim,
A gold-water Pactolus frets

Its brindled wharves and yellow brim,
The waxen colours weep and run
And slendering to his burning rim

Into the flat blue mist the sun
Drops out and all our day is done.

6 december

Speak of the North!
Charlotte Brontë (1816–1855)

Speak of the North! A lonely moor
Silent and dark and trackless swells,
The waves of some wild streamlet pour
Hurriedly through its ferny dells.

Profoundly still the twilight air,
Lifeless the landscape; so we deem,
Till like a phantom gliding near
A stag bends down to drink the stream.

And far away a mountain zone,
A cold, white waste of snow-drifts lies,
And one star, large and soft and lone,
Silently lights the unclouded skies.

7 december

The Owl and the Pussy-Cat
Edward Lear (1812–1888)

The Owl and the Pussy-cat went to sea
   In a beautiful pea-green boat;
They took some honey, and plenty of money
   Wrapped up in a five-pound note.
The Owl looked up to the stars above,
   And sang to a small guitar,
'O lovely Pussy! O Pussy, my love,
   What a beautiful Pussy you are,
      You are,
      You are!
What a beautiful Pussy you are!'

Pussy said to the Owl, 'You elegant fowl!
   How charmingly sweet you sing!
O let us be married! Too long we have tarried:
   But what shall we do for a ring?'
They sailed away, for a year and a day,
   To the land where the Bong-tree grows
And there in a wood a Piggy-wig stood
   With a ring at the end of his nose,
      His nose,
      His nose,
With a ring at the end of his nose.

[cont.]

'Dear Pig, are you willing to sell for one shilling
   Your ring?' Said the Piggy, 'I will.'
So they took it away, and were married next day
   By the Turkey who lives on the hill.
They dined on mince, and slices of quince,
   Which they ate with a runcible spoon;
And hand in hand, on the edge of the sand,
   They danced by the light of the moon,
      The moon,
      The moon,
They danced by the light of the moon.

8 december

The Post-Boy (extract)
William Cowper (1731–1800)

Now stir the fire, and close the shutters fast,
Let fall the curtains, wheel the sofa round,
And, while the bubbling and loud-hissing urn
Throws up a steamy column, and the cups,
That cheer but not inebriate, wait on each,
So let us welcome peaceful ev'ning in.

9 december

Late Fragment
Raymond Carver (1938–1988)

And did you get what
you wanted from this life, even so?
I did.
And what did you want?
To call myself beloved, to feel myself
beloved on the earth.

10 december

While We Sleep
Harold Monro (1879–1932)

The earth takes up our bodies, every one,
And brings them slowly backward to the dark;
Then on her shadowed side we droop and slumber,
Turned from the sun.

(Meanwhile, He covers continents in light
One after other, so they stretch and wake,
Live their day through and droop again to slumber:
Day, night: day, night.)

The stars shine forth and disappear again,
Roaring about in space above our heads,
While we are folded to the earth in slumber
With dreaming brain.

We travel through the darkness: we are spun
Upward through rays of light into the morning;
We waken with the earth: we glide from slumber
Toward the sun.

11 december

To Music, to Becalm his Fever (extract)
Robert Herrick (1591–1674)

Charm me asleep, and melt me so
  With thy delicious numbers,
That, being ravish'd, hence I go
  Away in easy slumbers.
    Ease my sick head,
    And make my bed,
Thou power that canst sever
  From me this ill,
  And quickly still,
  Though thou not kill
    My fever.

Thou sweetly canst convert the same
  From a consuming fire
Into a gentle licking flame,
  And make it thus expire.
    Then make me weep
    My pains asleep;
And give me such reposes
  That I, poor I,
  May think thereby
  I live and die
    'Mongst roses.

12 december

Desiderata
Max Ehrmann (1872-1945)

Go placidly amid the noise and haste,
and remember what peace there may be in silence.
As far as possible without surrender
be on good terms with all persons;
Speak your truth quietly and clearly;
and listen to others,
even the dull and the ignorant;
they too have their story.
Avoid loud and aggressive persons;
they are vexations to the spirit.
If you compare yourself with others,
you may become vain and bitter;
for always there will be greater and lesser persons than yourself.
Enjoy your achievements as well as your plans.
Keep interested in your own career, however humble;
it is a real possession in the changing fortunes of time.
Exercise caution in your business affairs;
for the world is full of trickery.
But let this not blind you to what virtue there is;
many persons strive for high ideals;
and everywhere life is full of heroism.
Be yourself.
Especially, do not feign affection.
Neither be cynical about love;
for in the face of all aridity and disenchantment
it is as perennial as the grass.

[cont.]

Take kindly the counsel of the years,
gracefully surrendering the things of youth.
Nurture strength of spirit to shield you in sudden misfortune.
But do not distress yourself with dark imaginings.
Many fears are born of fatigue and loneliness.
Beyond a wholesome discipline,
be gentle with yourself.
You are a child of the universe,
no less than the trees and the stars;
you have a right to be here.
And whether or not it is clear to you,
no doubt the universe is unfolding as it should.
Therefore be at peace with God,
whatever you conceive Him to be,
and whatever your labors and aspirations,
in the noisy confusion of life keep peace with your soul.
With all its sham, drudgery, and broken dreams,
it is still a beautiful world.
Be cheerful.
Strive to be happy.

13 december

In the Mid-Midwinter
after John Donne's 'A Nocturnal on St Lucy's Day'
Liz Lochhead (b. 1947)

At midday on the year's midnight
into my mind came
I saw the new moon late yestreen
wi the auld moon in her airms
though, no,
there is no moon of course –
there's nothing very much of anything to speak of
in the sky except a gey dreich greyness
rain-laden over Glasgow and today
there is the very least of even this for us to get
but
the light comes back
the light always comes back
and this begins tomorrow with
however many minutes more of sun and serotonin.

Meanwhile
there will be the winter moon for us to love the longest,
fat in the frosty sky among the sharpest stars,
and lines of old songs we can't remember
why we know
or when first we heard them
will aye come back
once in a blue moon to us
unbidden

and bless us with their long-travelled light.

14 december

The Earthly Paradise (extract)
William Morris *(1834–1896)*

   Dreamer of dreams, born out of my due time,
Why should I strive to set the crooked straight?
Let it suffice me that my murmuring rhyme
Beats with light wing against the ivory gate,
Telling a tale not too importunate
To those who in the sleepy region stay,
Lulled by the singer of an empty day.

   Folk say, a wizard to a northern king
At Christmas-tide such wondrous things did show,
That through one window men beheld the spring,
And through another saw the summer glow,
And through a third the fruited vines a-row,
While still, unheard, but in its wonted way,
Piped the drear wind of that December day.

   So with this Earthly Paradise it is,
If ye will read aright, and pardon me,
Who strive to build a shadowy isle of bliss
Midmost the beating of the steely sea,
Where tossed about all hearts of men must be;
Whose ravening monsters mighty men shall slay,
Not the poor singer of an empty day.

15 december

A Hope
Charles Kingsley (1819–1875)

Twin stars, aloft in ether clear,
Around each other roll alway,
Within one common atmosphere
Of their own mutual light and day.

And myriad happy eyes are bent
Upon their changeless love alway;
As, strengthened by their one intent,
They pour the flood of life and day.

So we through this world's waning night
May, hand in hand, pursue our way;
Shed round us order, love, and light,
And shine unto the perfect day.

16 december

Ode to Winter
Gillian Clarke (b. 1937)

We hoard light, hunkered in holt and burrow,
in cave, *cwtsh*, den, earth, hut, lair.
Sun blinks. Trees take down their hair.
Dusk wipes horizons, seeps into the room,
the last flame of geranium in the gloom.

In the shortening day, bring in the late flowers
to crisp in a vase, beech to break into leaf,
a branch of lark. Take winter by the throat.
Feed the common birds, tits and finches,
the spotted woodpecker in his opera coat.

Let's learn to love the icy winter moon,
or moonless dark and winter constellations,
Jupiter's glow, a slow, incoming plane,
neighbourly windows, someone's flickering screen,
a lamp-lit page, drawn curtains.

Let us praise intimacy, talk and books,
music and silence, wind and rain,
the beautiful bones of trees, taste of cold air,
darkening fields, the glittering city,
that winter longing, *hiraeth*, something like prayer.

Under the stilled heartbeat of trees,
wind-snapped branches, mulch and root,
a million bluebell bulbs lie low
ready to flare in lengthening light,
after the dark, the frozen earth, the snow.

Out there, fox and buzzard, kite and crow
are clearing the ground for the myth.
On the darkest day bring in the tree,
cool and pungent as forest. Turn up the music.
Pour us a glass. Dress the house in pagan finery.

17 december

Night
William Morris (1834–1896)

I am Night: I bring again
Hope of pleasure, rest from pain:
Thoughts unsaid 'twixt Life and Death
My fruitful silence quickeneth.

18 december

Night Rhapsody (extract)
Robert Nichols (1893–1944)

How beautiful it is to wake at night,
When over all there reigns the ultimate spell
Of complete silence, darkness absolute,
To feel the world, tilted on axle-tree,
In slow gyration, with no sensible sound,
Unless to ears of unimagined beings,
Resident incorporeal or stretched
In vigilance of ecstasy among
Ethereal paths and the celestial maze.
The rumour of our onward course now brings
A steady rustle, as of some strange ship
Darkling with soundless sail all set and amply filled
By volume of an ever-constant air,
At fullest night, through seas for ever calm,
Swept lovely and unknown for ever on.

19 december

Deck the Halls
Traditional

Deck the halls with boughs of holly,
'Tis the season to be jolly,
Don we now our gay apparel,
Troll the ancient Yuletide carol.

See the blazing Yule before us,
Strike the harp and join the chorus,
Follow me in merry measure,
While I tell of Yuletide treasure.

Fast away the old year passes,
Hail the new, ye lads and lasses,
Sing we joyous all together,
Heedless of the wind and weather.

20 december

O Little Town of Bethlehem
Phillips Brooks (1835-1893)

O little town of Bethlehem
How still we see thee lie!
Above thy deep and dreamless sleep
The silent stars go by.
Yet in thy dark streets shineth
The everlasting light
The hopes and fears of all the years
Are met in thee tonight.

O morning stars, together
Proclaim the holy birth,
And praises sing to God the King
And peace to men on earth;
For Christ is born of Mary;
And, gathered all above,
While mortals sleep, the angels keep
Their watch of wondering love.

How silently, how silently,
The wondrous gift is given!
So God imparts to human hearts
The blessings of his heaven.
No ear may hear his coming;
But in this world of sin,
Where meek souls will receive him, still
The dear Christ enters in.

[cont.]

Where children pure and happy
Pray to the blessed child,
Where misery cries out to thee,
Son of the mother mild;
Where charity stands watching
And faith holds wide the door,
The dark night wakes, the glory breaks,
And Christmas comes once more.

O holy Child of Bethlehem
Descend to us we pray;
Cast out our sin, and enter in,
Be born in us today.
We hear the Christmas angels
The great glad tidings tell:
O come to us, abide with us;
Our Lord Emmanuel.

21 december

Stopping by Woods on a Snowy Evening
Robert Frost (1874-1963)

Whose woods these are I think I know.
His house is in the village though;
He will not see me stopping here
To watch his woods fill up with snow.

My little horse must think it queer
To stop without a farmhouse near
Between the woods and frozen lake
The darkest evening of the year.

He gives his harness bells a shake
To ask if there is some mistake.
The only other sound's the sweep
Of easy wind and downy flake.

The woods are lovely, dark and deep,
But I have promises to keep,
And miles to go before I sleep,
And miles to go before I sleep.

22 december

The Wise Men
Nancy Anne Miller

The wise men waited their turn,
used to the sky's slow messages of
night-brailled stars. Shot in slurred
light years, across a silence so vast
one had to be guided. This one

heavy star, swollen with a glow,
hung in its own path, like a bridal
veil pinned, invited the three guests,
steady with gifts. Reluctant to hurry,
until they bore the holy ache of awe.

23 december

A Child's Christmas in Wales (extract)
Dylan Thomas (1914-1953)

Looking through my bedroom window, out into the moonlight and unending smoke-coloured snow, I could see the lights in the windows of all the other houses on our hill and hear the music rising from them up the long, steadily falling night. I turned the gas down, I got into bed. I said some words to the close and holy darkness, and then I slept.

24 december

A Visit from St Nicholas
Clement Clarke Moore (1779-1863)

Twas the night before Christmas, when all through the house
Not a creature was stirring, not even a mouse;
The stockings were hung by the chimney with care,
In hopes that St Nicholas soon would be there;
The children were nestled all snug in their beds;
While visions of sugar-plums danced in their heads;
And mamma in her kerchief, and I in my cap,
Had just settled our brains for a long winter's nap –
When out on the lawn there arose such a clatter,
I sprang from my bed to see what was the matter.
Away to the window I flew like a flash,
Tore open the shutters and threw up the sash.
The moon on the breast of the new-fallen snow,
Gave a lustre of midday to objects below;
When what to my wondering eyes did appear,
But a miniature sleigh and eight tiny reindeer,
With a little old driver so lively and quick,
I knew in a moment it must be St Nick.
More rapid than eagles his coursers they came,
And he whistled, and shouted, and called them by name:
'Now, *Dasher*! now, *Dancer*! now, *Prancer* and *Vixen*!
On, *Comet*! on, *Cupid*! on, *Doner* and *Blitzen*!
To the top of the porch! to the top of the wall!
Now dash away! dash away! dash away all!'
As leaves that before the wild hurricane fly,
When they meet with an obstacle, mount to the sky;
So up to the house-top the coursers they flew
With the sleigh full of toys, and St Nicholas too –

And then, in a twinkling I heard on the roof
The prancing and pawing of each little hoof.
As I drew in my head, and was turning around,
Down the chimney St Nicholas came with a bound.
He was dressed all in fur, from his head to his foot,
And his clothes were all tarnished with ashes and soot;
A bundle of toys he had flung on his back,
And he looked like a pedlar just opening his pack.
His eyes – how they twinkled! his dimples, how merry!
His cheeks were like roses, his nose like a cherry!
His droll little mouth was drawn up like a bow,
And the beard on his chin was as white as the snow;
The stump of a pipe he held tight in his teeth,
And the smoke, it encircled his head like a wreath;
He had a broad face and a little round belly
That shook, when he laughed, like a bowl full of jelly.
He was chubby and plump, a right jolly old elf,
And I laughed when I saw him, in spite of myself;
A wink of his eye and a twist of his head
Soon gave me to know I had nothing to dread;
He spoke not a word, but went straight to his work,
And filled all the stockings; then turned with a jerk,
And laying his finger aside of his nose,
And giving a nod, up the chimney he rose;
He sprang to his sleigh, to his team gave a whistle,
And away they all flew like the down of a thistle.
But I heard him exclaim, ere he drove out of sight:
'Happy Christmas to all, and to all a good night!'

25 december

'It came upon the midnight clear'
Edmund Hamilton Sears (1810–1876)

It came upon the midnight clear,
   That glorious song of old,
From angels bending near the earth
   To touch their harps of gold:
'Peace on the earth, good will to men,
   From heaven's all-gracious King!'
The world in solemn stillness lay
   To hear the angels sing.

Still through the cloven skies they come,
   With peaceful wings unfurled;
And still their heavenly music floats
   O'er all the weary world:
Above its sad and lowly plains
   They bend on hovering wing;
And ever o'er its Babel-sounds
   The blessed angels sing.

Yet with the woes of sin and strife
   The world has suffered long;
Beneath the angel-strain have rolled
   Two thousand years of wrong;
And man, at war with man, hears not
   The love-song which they bring:
O hush the noise, ye men of strife,
   And hear the angels sing.

For lo, the days are hastening on,
  By prophet-bards foretold,
When, with the ever-circling years,
  Comes round the age of gold;
When peace shall over all the earth
  Its ancient splendours fling,
And the whole world give back the song
  Which now the angels sing.

26 december

A Winter Evening
***Alexander Pushkin (1799-1837),
translated by Martha Dickinson Bianchi***

Sable clouds by tempest driven,
Snowflakes whirling in the gales,
Hark – it sounds like grim wolves howling,
Hark – now like a child it wails!
Creeping through the rustling straw thatch,
Rattling on the mortared walls,
Like some weary wanderer knocking –
On the lowly pane it falls.

Fearsome darkness fills the kitchen,
Drear and lonely our retreat,
Speak a word and break the silence,
Dearest little Mother, sweet!
Has the moaning of the tempest
Closed thine eyelids wearily?
Has the spinning wheel's soft whirring
Hummed a cradle song to thee?

Sweetheart of my youthful Springtime,
Thou true-souled companion dear –
Let us drink! Away with sadness!
Wine will fill our hearts with cheer.
Sing the song how free and careless
Birds live in a distant land –
Sing the song of maids at morning
Meeting by the brook's clear strand!

Sable clouds by tempest driven,
Snowflakes whirling in the gales,
Hark – it sounds like grim wolves howling,
Hark – now like a child it wails!
Sweetheart of my youthful Springtime,
Thou true-souled companion dear,
Let us drink! Away with sadness!
Wine will fill our hearts with cheer!

27 december

Address to a Child During a Boisterous
Winter Evening (extract)
Dorothy Wordsworth (1771–1855)

What way does the wind come? What way does he go?
He rides over the water, and over the snow,
Through wood, and through vale; and o'er rocky height,
Which the goat cannot climb, takes his sounding flight;
He tosses about in every bare tree,
As, if you look up, you may plainly see;
But how he will come, and whither he goes,
There's never a scholar in England knows.

Hark! over the roof he makes a pause,
And growls as if he would fix his claws
Right in the slates, and with a huge rattle
Drive them down, like men in a battle:
– But let him range round; he does us no harm,
We build up the fire, we're snug and warm;
Untouched by his breath see the candle shines bright,
And burns with a clear and steady light.

Books have we to read, but that half-stifled knell,
Alas! 'tis the sound of the eight o'clock bell.
– Come, now we'll to bed! and when we are there
He may work his own will, and what shall we care?
He may knock at the door – we'll not let him in;
May drive at the windows – we'll laugh at his din;
Let him seek his own home wherever it be;
Here's a *cozie* warm house for Edward and me.

28 december

The Seasons (extract)
James Thomson (1700-1748)

Through the hushed air the whitening shower descends,
At first thin-wavering; till at last the flakes
Fall broad and wide and fast, dimming the day,
With a continual flow. The cherished fields
Put on their winter robe of purest white.
'Tis brightness all; save where the new snow melts
Along the mazy current. Low the woods
Bow their hoar heads; and, ere the languid sun
Faint from the west emits his evening ray,
Earth's universal face, deep-hid and chill,
Is one wild, dazzling waste.

29 december

I Had a Boat
Mary Elizabeth Coleridge (1861-1907)

I had a boat, and the boat had wings;
   And I did dream that we went a flying
Over the heads of queens and kings,
   Over the souls dead and dying,
Up among the stars and the great white rings,
   And where the Moon on her back is lying.

30 december

The Year
Ella Wheeler Wilcox (1850-1919)

What can be said in New Year rhymes,
That's not been said a thousand times?

The new years come, the old years go,
We know we dream, we dream we know.

We rise up laughing with the light,
We lie down weeping with the night.

We hug the world until it stings,
We curse it then and sigh for wings.

We live, we love, we woo, we wed,
We wreathe our prides, we sheet our dead.

We laugh, we weep, we hope, we fear,
And that's the burden of a year.

31 december

Auld Lang Syne
Robert Burns (1759-1796)

Should auld acquaintance be forgot
    And never brought to mind?
Should auld acquaintance be forgot,
    And auld lang syne!

For auld lang syne, my jo,
    For auld lang syne,
We'll tak a cup o'kindness yet
    For auld lang syne.

And surely ye'll be your pint stowp!
    And surely I'll be mine!
And we'll tak a cup o'kindness yet,
    For auld lang syne.

For auld lang syne, my jo, ...

We twa hae run about the braes
    And pou'd the gowans fine;
But we've wander'd many a weary fitt,
    Sin auld lang syne.

For auld lang syne, my jo, ...

We twa hae paidl'd in the burn
    Frae morning sun till dine;
But seas between us braid hae roar'd,
    Sin auld lang syne.

For auld lang syne, my jo, …

And there's a hand, my trusty fiere!
    And gie's a hand o' thine!
And we'll tak a right gude-willie-waught,
    For auld lang syne

For auld lang syne, my jo, …

Acknowledgements

The poems in this anthology are reprinted from the following books, all by permission of the publishers listed unless stated otherwise. Every effort has been made to trace the copyright holders of the poems published in this book. The editor and publisher apologise if any material has been included without permission or without the appropriate acknowledgement and would be glad to be told of anyone who has not been consulted.

Thanks are due to all the copyright holders cited below for their kind permission:

Wendell Berry, *The Peace of Wild Things: and Other Poems* (Penguin Books, 2018) by permission of Penguin Random House UK.

Helen Burke, *Today the Birds Will Sing: Collected Poems* (Valley Press, 2017) by permission of the publisher on behalf of the Estate of Helen Burke.

Moya Cannon, *Collected Poems* (Carcanet Press, 2021).

Nicola Davies, Dom Conlon and James Carter, *Out There in the Wild: Poems on Nature* (Macmillan Children's Books, 2023) by permission of PLS Clear.

Raymond Carver, *All of Us: The Collected Poems* (Harvill Press, 1996) by permission of International Creative Management Inc.

Gillian Clarke, *Collected Poems* (Carcanet Press, 1997).

Dom Conlon, *Watcher of the Skies: Poems about Space and Aliens*, ed. Emma Wright & Rachel Piercey (The Emma Press, 2016), p. 54 – by permission of the poet: dom@domconlon.com.

Wendy Cope, *Family Values* (Faber & Faber, 2012).

John F. Deane, *Selected and New Poems* (Carcanet Press, 2023).

Peter Didsbury, *Scenes from a Long Sleep: New & Collected Poems* (Bloodaxe, 2003) www.bloodaxebooks.com.

Rita Dove, *On the Bus with Rosa Parks: Poems* (W. W. Norton, 1999).

Carol Ann Duffy, *New and Collected Poems for Children* (Faber & Faber, 2009) by permission of the author c/o Rogers, Coleridge & White.

Vona Groarke, *Flight and Earlier Poems* (Gallery Press, 2004) by permission of Gallery Press.

Salena Godden, *With Love, Grief & Fury* (Canongate Books, 2024) by permission of PLS Clear.

Langston Hughes, *The Norton Anthology of Poetry* (W.W. Norton, 2005), p. 1431 – by permission of Alfred A. Knopf, a division of Random House Inc, and Harold Ober Associates.

Kathleen Jamie, *Jizzen* (Picador, 1999) by permission of the author.

Jaan Kaplinski, *Selected Poems* (Bloodaxe Books, 2011) www.bloodaxebooks.com.

Galway Kinnell, *Selected Poems* (Houghton Mifflin USA, 2000; Bloodaxe Books, 2001) www.bloodaxebooks.com.

Liz Lochhead, *Fugitive Colours* (Birlinn Limited, 2017) by permission of PLS Clear.

Derek Mahon, *New Collected Poems* (Gallery Books, 2011) by permission of The Gallery Press.

Nancy Anne Miller, *Queen Palm: A Bermuda Christmas* (Valley Press, 2023).

Edwin Morgan, *Collected Poems* (Carcanet Press, 1996).

Naomi Shihab Nye, *Words Under the Words: Selected Poems* (The Eighth Mountain Press, USA, 1994).

P. K. Page, *The Hidden Room: Collected Poems*, Volume 2 (The Porcupine's Quill, Canada, 1997).

Sheenagh Pugh, *Beware Falling Tortoises* (Poetry Wales Press, 1987) by permission of Poetry Wales Ltd.

Lemn Sissay, *Let the Light Pour In: Morning Poems* (Canongate Books, 2023) by permission of C&W Agency.

Clare Shaw, poem first appeared in *Christmas Movies* (Candlestick Press, 2021), p. 7 – by permission of the poet.

Kathryn Simmonds, *Scenes from Life on Earth* (Salt Publishing, 2022).

Mark Strand, *Selected Poems* (Alfred A. Knopf, 1979) by permission of Alfred A. Knopf, an imprint of Knopf Doubleday, a division of Penguin Random House LLC, and the Wylie Agency.

Rebecca Swift, *A Suitable Love Object* (Valley Press, 2020) by permission of the publisher on behalf of the Estate of Rebecca Swift.

Henri Thomas, *Into the Deep Street: Seven Modern French Poets 1938-2008*, tr. by Jennie Feldman and Stephen Romer (Anvil Press Poetry, 2009). Original French poem from *Travaux d'Aveugle* (Éditions Gallimard, Paris, 1941). By permission of both publisher and translators.

Sarah Watkinson, *Photovoltaic: Love Songs to Greenery from a Poet-Scientist* (Valley Press, 2024).

James Wright, *Saint Judas* (Wesleyan University Press, 1959).

Belinda Zhawi, poem commissioned by BBC Radio 3's *Late Junction* and used here by kind permission of the author.

All permissions were cleared courtesy of Dr Suzanne Fairless-Aitken c/o Swift Permissions: swiftpermissions@gmail.com.

'I will arise and go now, for always night and day
I hear lake water lapping with low sounds by the shore;
While I stand on the roadway, or on the pavements grey,
I hear it in the deep heart's core.'
W. B. Yeats (1865–1939)